NAPOLEON
BONAPARTE

LEADERSHIP ▪ STRATEGY ▪ CONFLICT

GREGORY FREMONT-BARNES

First published in Great Britain in 2010 by Osprey Publishing,
Midland House, West Way, Botley, Oxford OX2 0PH, UK
44-02 23rd St, Suite 219, Long Island City, NY 11101, USA

E-mail: info@ospreypublishing.com

A CIP catalogue record for this book is available from the British
Library.

ISBN: 978 1 84603 458 9

Editorial by Ilios Publishing Ltd, Oxford, UK
(www.iliospublishing.com)
Page layout by Myriam Bell Design, France
Index by Sandra Shotter
Typeset in 1 Stone Serif and Officina Sans ITC Standard
Maps by Mapping Specialists Ltd
Originated by PDQ Media, Bungay, UK
Printed in China through Worldprint Ltd

10 11 12 13 14   10 9 8 7 6 5 4 3 2 1

Dedication

This book is dedicated to my older son, William, whose peaceful
disposition inclines him to conquer with pen rather than with sword.

Artist's note

Readers may care to note that the original paintings from which the
colour plates in this book were prepared are available for private sale.
The Publishers retain all reproduction copyright whatsoever.
All enquiries should be addressed to:

Peter Dennis, Fieldhead, The Park, Mansfield, Notts, NG18 2AT, UK

The Publishers regret that they can enter into no correspondence
upon this matter.

The Woodland Trust

Osprey Publishing are supporting the Woodland Trust, the UK's
leading woodland conservation charity, by funding the dedication
of trees.

FOR A CATALOGUE OF ALL BOOKS PUBLISHED BY OSPREY
MILITARY AND AVIATION PLEASE CONTACT:

Osprey Direct, c/o Random House Distribution Center,
400 Hahn Road, Westminster, MD 21157
Email: uscustomerservice@ospreypublishing.com

Osprey Direct, The Book Service Ltd, Distribution Centre,
Colchester Road, Frating Green, Colchester, Essex, CO7 7DW
E-mail: customerservice@ospreypublishing.com

www.ospreypublishing.com

CONTENTS

Napoleon in 1813. Even
while at bay in the latter
years from this period,
the Emperor displayed
remarkable skill in
harnessing increasingly
scarce resources of men,
horses, weapons and
supplies. Yet no capacity
for administrative – not
to mention tactical – skill,
no matter how impressive,
could account for his
achievements without
appreciating the
extraordinary domestic
popularity he enjoyed.
(Author's collection)

INTRODUCTION

With the possible exception of Alexander, Napoleon justifiably ranks as history's greatest commander. As a strategist he had few equals, favouring brief, sharp campaigns in which he sought to outmanoeuvre his opponent and bring him to battle at a place and time of his choosing. His masterful understanding of strategy proved consistently successful between 1796 and 1809, and as late as his final campaign, culminating at Waterloo, he seized the initiative and manoeuvred his army at remarkable speed, catching his opponents unprepared. Napoleon's rise was nothing if not meteoric. From a mere captain he reached the rank of brigadier-general in the course of eight weeks. By 1796 he had attained the rank of army commander, partly by exhibiting the military qualities and skills required, but also through political opportunism. Three years later, in 1799, he assumed power as First Consul, making him de facto ruler of France. Five years later, at the age of 35, he was crowned emperor, and between 1805 and 1812 he conquered much of Europe, only to see his empire gradually collapse from 1813, his abdication forced in 1814, before a brief return to power in 1815.

In the course of these two decades in the field, Napoleon revolutionized warfare. Gone were the days of confronting a strong position, laying methodical siege and manoeuvring in the field until, once the advantage lay clearly with one side, a negotiated peace could be arranged, with limited concessions granted and no decisive outcome achieved. Napoleon eschewed all this, attacking the flanks and rear of the opposing army and those features that the great Prussian military theorist Carl von Clausewitz would later call the 'centre of gravity'. Hereafter, Napoleon would bypass

fortresses, making straight for the enemy's main force, the destruction of which would bring about a swift and successful conclusion to the campaign.

Yet while perfecting the principles that govern strategy and tactics, as well as demonstrating that finesse which renders warfare as much a form of art as a science, he also committed blunders on a grand strategic scale – some truly catastrophic. His grand scheme for the economic collapse of his most inveterate enemy, Britain, proved fatally counter-productive, harming the French economy and alienating the population of the Empire's satellite states, whose livelihoods suffered by the imposition of an embargo impossible to enforce and which they made every effort to circumvent. In turn, by attempting to impose his will over Portugal, a nation reluctant to cooperate in this scheme, Napoleon became drawn into a long and ultimately exceedingly costly conflict in Iberia, where the constant drain on men and resources slowly sapped the Empire while Napoleon faced more formidable opponents elsewhere. His invasion of Russia in 1812, another by-product of his desire to strike at Great Britain by indirect means, laid the foundation for his ultimate downfall.

THE EARLY YEARS

Napoleon Bonaparte, the son of an impoverished Corsican count, was born Napoleone Buonaparte in Ajaccio on 15 August 1769, the year after the Genoese lost the island to France, and the second son of the eight children of Carlo Buonaparte and Maria Letizia Ramolino Buonaparte. By chance, circumstances were changing for Corsica, and Napoleon's family found themselves caught up in a critical period. His parents had supported the Corsican patriot, Pasquale Paoli, against Genoese rule and by the time Paoli was defeated by Genoese forces, Letizia was pregnant with Napoleon. Genoa however soon ceded the island to France, making the newborn a subject of the King of France, with the family's distant claims to noble

The house in which Napoleon was born, 15 August 1769, in Ajaccio, on the west coast of Corsica. It has been a museum since 1923. (Author's collection)

status confirmed by the Bourbon government. Still, if the Buonapartes were not impoverished, neither were they wealthy, and Napoleon's father eked out a humble living as a lawyer until his death in 1785, all the while cultivating ties with French officials on the island with the express purpose of sending his children to the mainland for their education.

Accordingly, in January 1779, Napoleon and his older brother Giuseppe (later changed to Joseph) were packed off to boarding school at Autun, where the nine-year-old

Napoleon at the military academy at Brienne, c.1785. A product of the Corsican *petite noblesse*, he had enough money and influence to procure a state education under the Bourbon regime without being hamstrung by exalted social position which would have barred him from the opportunities that the coming Revolution offered. As such, he enjoyed the good fortune of coming of age during a period of great social and political upheaval. (Author's collection)

Napoleon received his first taste of a military education and ceased to use the final 'e' in his Christian name in an effort to integrate himself more closely into French society. If his pedigree did not amount to much in the eyes of his schoolmates on the mainland, it nevertheless qualified him for a free place in April 1779 as a cadet to l'École Royale at Brienne, where he was known for the fierce manner in which he espoused Corsican nationalism and demonstrated a strong capacity in mathematics. In October 1784 he moved to the École Militaire in Paris, receiving his commission as a second lieutenant in the artillery in September 1785. There his teachers found him very studious and extremely ambitious, traits perhaps reflecting a sense of inferiority in the light of his position as a foreigner from a modestly endowed provincial family, and speaking with an accent that strongly betrayed his Corsican upbringing.

Between 1785 and 1791 Napoleon served with the Régiment de la Fère at Valence and then at the École d'Artillerie at Auxonne, and as such did not witness the major events of the French Revolution at close hand, though he did take a keen interest in their progress. In 1789, the *ancien régime* under Louis XVI, facing a serious financial crisis partly born out of the vast expenses incurred by supporting the American rebels during their recent war of independence against Great Britain, was obliged to raise taxes whose extent required the convening of the representatives of the Estates General, a legislative body that had not sat in session since 1614 – a fact which alone speaks volumes for the power of the 18th-century French monarchy. The meeting sparked a constitutional crisis, and on 14 July 1789 a mob stormed the Bastille, the notorious Parisian fortress and prison which had come to symbolize not merely royalist authority but also tyranny, thus inaugurating a revolution that quickly established a constitutional monarchy, retaining Louis as head of state but substantially curbing his powers. For young officers like Napoleon, these developments proved exceptionally providential, for the abolition of noble privileges in the army created vacancies in the ranks of junior officers by those who fled France or remained and later found themselves at the foot of the guillotine, so clearing the path to promotion for those ambitious and talented enough to seize opportunities hitherto barred to men outside the narrow world of the upper classes.

With the attentions of Prussia, Russia and Austria engaged elsewhere and with Britain not yet perceiving her interests threatened by the altered political state across the Channel, France remained at peace during the early years of the Revolution. Following leave in Corsica, Napoleon was promoted, first lieutenant in April 1792 and captain the following month. An adherent of Jacobinism, popular government and centralization, he was present in Paris when a Parisian crowd attacked the Tuileries palace on 10 August and overthrew the king, proclaiming a republic on 22 September. That month Napoleon returned to Corsica, where he opposed in the Jacobin clubs the movement begun by Paoli for independence from French rule. Affairs in Corsica grew from bad to worse, with open revolt occurring in March 1793. Napoleon's entire clan fled immediately and took refuge on the mainland.

Attack on the Bastille fortress and prison, 14 July 1789. The event, which traditionally marks the outbreak of the French Revolution, not only led to the eventual deposition of the king and the establishment of a republic, but created a meritocratic environment in which many young officers, most notably Napoleon, could propel themselves to potentially meteoric heights despite their humble origins. (Author's collection)

His time in Corsica had prevented Napoleon from taking a share in the remarkable French victory over the Prussians at Valmy in September 1792, but by adhering to the Jacobin party he ensured for the moment his political reliability during a period when enemies of the state – real or perceived – found themselves facing execution in large numbers. The new French Government dominated by Maximilien Robespierre, known as the Convention, exercised harsh justice from the very beginning of its administration in July 1793, in a period that came ominously to be known as the Terror. Quite apart from organizing the defence of France against a coalition of enemies consisting of Austria, Prussia, Great Britain, Holland, Spain and a host of lesser powers, the Convention faced internal threats posed by royalist supporters, most notably in the Vendée to the west and in Marseille and Toulon in the south.

THE MILITARY LIFE

It was in fact in Toulon where Napoleon first made his name on the military stage as a 24-year-old captain of artillery during the siege of that vital port city at the end of 1793, when the royalist population raised the banner of revolt against the Republic and called for British aid. A Royal Navy fleet duly arrived and disembarked a small force of British troops and sailors who, in conjunction with poor-quality troops from Spain, Sardinia and Naples, soon found themselves perilously invested along a perimeter of 16km (10 miles) by 38,000 Republican troops. At the same time they grappled with the problem of the now harbour-bound French fleet, which declared itself for the Republic. By chance Napoleon had been posted to the siege as a consequence of a fellow officer falling wounded, so rendering the young captain impromptu commander of the artillery. With no combat experience but a natural talent for surveying and appreciating ground, he determined that by capturing a single enemy position, known as Fort Mulgrave, the French would command

Napoleon at the siege of Toulon, December 1793. As a result of a two-day bombardment from batteries directed by the young captain, the British fleet was forced to withdraw, enabling Republican forces to retake the port city and massacre its royalist inhabitants. (Author's collection)

such a prominent presence above the port as to render the anchorage untenable and force the Anglo-Spanish fleet to withdraw, abandoning rebellious Toulon to its fate.

The newly promoted Major Bonaparte began to implement his plan in mid-November, and after three weeks concentrating the necessary guns, he began a two-day bombardment on 15 December. On the 17th, 6,000 Republican troops, led by Napoleon, seized the fort with no resistance offered by its Spanish garrison, which evaporated before the onslaught. The following day the Allies evacuated the city, burning many vessels but still leaving behind much of the enemy fleet intact. Napoleon's success at Toulon marked the beginning of his meteoric rise; the new government, known as the Directory, found him useful when food riots began to grip Paris and a right-wing coup developed on 4–5 October 1795 (known in the revolutionary calendar as 13 Vendémiaire). Now a *général de brigade*, Napoleon deployed artillery in the street and administered his famous 'whiff of grapeshot', bringing a swift and bloody end to the attempted coup and earning for himself a promotion to *général de division* and command of the Armée de l'Intérieur.

Yet Napoleon desired more than this as compensation for an act that had saved his political masters, who themselves probably balked at the idea that so remarkable a young general should remain in such close proximity to the seat of power; as such he was given command of the Armée de l'Italie on 2 March 1796. The campaign in northern Italy was meant as a subsidiary one against the Austrians and their Piedmontese allies. Napoleon, in charge of 63,000 troops, was expected to defeat the Piedmontese before driving the Austrians back across Lombardy as far as the Adige. Subsequent operations were meant to bring him into the mountainous Tyrol, there to meet with General Moreau coming from the south. Prospects on the Italian front were not good, but Napoleon married the beautiful Joséphine de Beauharnais and arrived at headquarters on 26 March, eager to make a name for himself.

The Armée de l'Italie held a position extending between Genoa and Nice, but in reality with only 37,000 men fit for duty. Even these were in poor condition

Napoleon's principal campaigns

Napoleon's principal campaigns, 1796–1815
(as depicted on a map of 1810)

④ Campaign location

Under direct rule by Napoleon

Under rule by members of Napoleon's family

Dependent state

0 — 400 miles
0 — 400 km

(1) First and Second Italian campaigns (1796–97, 1800)

12 April 1796	Montenotte
14–15 April	Dego
21 April	Mondovi
8 May	Fombio
10 May	Lodi
30 May	Borghetto
3 August	Lonato
5 August	Castiglione
8 September	Bassano
12 November	Caldiero
15–17 November	Arcola
14 January 1797	Rivoli
14 June 1800	Marengo

(2) Middle East campaign (1798–99)

2 July 1798	Alexandria
21 July	Pyramids
7 March 1799	Jaffa
18 March–20 May	Acre (siege)
17 April	Mount Tabor
25 July	Aboukir

(3) 1805 campaign

2 December	Austerlitz

(4) 1806 campaign

14 October	Jena

(5) 1807 campaign

7–8 February	Eylau
10 June	Heilsberg
14 June	Friedland

(6) 1809 campaign

19/20 April	Abensberg
21 April	Landshut
23 April	Ratisbon
21–22 May	Aspern-Essling
5–6 July	Wagram
10 July	Znaim

(7) Spanish campaign (1808)

30 November	Somosierra

(8) Russian campaign (1812)

28 July	Vitebsk
17 August	Smolensk
19 August	Valutino
7 September	Borodino
16–17 November	Krasnyi
26–28 November	Berezina

(9) 1813 campaign

2 May	Lützen
20–21 May	Bautzen
26–27 August	Dresden
16–19 October	Leipzig
30–31 October	Hanau

(10) 1814 campaign

29 January	Brienne
30 January	La Rothière
10 February	Champaubert
11 February	Montmirail
12 February	Château-Thierry
14 February	Vauchamps
18 February	Montereau
27 February	Bar-sur-Aube
7 March	Craonne
9–10 March	Lâon
13 March	Reims
20–21 March	Arcis-sur-Aube

(11) Waterloo campaign (1815)

16 June	Ligny
18 June	Waterloo

and woefully equipped, lacking in some cases boots and even muskets. Transport consisted of only a few hundred mules, with men subsisting on reduced rations, and horses and pack animals suffering from a serious shortage of fodder. With pay weeks in arrears and signs of mutiny everywhere, the new commander had his work cut out. By now the army had received sufficient training so that it could fight and manoeuvre in line as well as in column, to which Napoleon introduced his favourite formation, the *ordre mixte* – consisting of anything from a single battalion to an entire brigade deployed in line, its flanks protected by a formation of equal strength but arrayed in column, thus providing this combined unit with the advantages of both the firepower of a line at its centre and the impetus and solidity of a column.

Napoleon's 'whiff of grapeshot', in which he cleared away a Parisian mob during the counter-revolutionary uprising of 13 Vendémiaire (5 October 1795). This episode, which marked the captain of artillery's debut on the Parisian political scene, preserved the new government, known as the Directory, from almost certain overthrow. (Author's collection)

Napoleon attacked the junction between the two opposing armies of generals Colli and Argenteau on 12 April, destroying the latter's right at Montenotte so thoroughly as to leave only 700 out of 6,000 men remaining. In so doing Napoleon interposed his troops between the Piedmontese and the Austrians, thus introducing one of the key traits so characteristic of his later campaigns – dividing separate elements of a numerically superior enemy in order to defeat their smaller, constituent parts in detail. Napoleon then launched separate divisions against the Piedmontese and Austrians, driving them further apart, the latter being defeated at Dego on 14 August. He then concentrated his entire force against the now-isolated Piedmontese, and routed them at Mondovi on the 21st. Having now reached the plains and with nothing to halt his march on Turin, Napoleon received terms for an armistice from Colli. In little more than a fortnight he had achieved a score of victories, inflicted 25,000 casualties, captured over 50 guns and knocked the Piedmontese out of the war. Napoleon was no longer an obscure general, but the most prominent in Europe.

Now reinforced to 40,000 men, he pursued Beaulieu, who was obliged to withdraw eastwards in haste, crossing the river Adda and leaving a rearguard at Lodi in the vain hope of delaying the French advance. Napoleon crushed the rearguard in a battle that was to become central to the 'Napoleonic myth'. The battle came to symbolize the seemingly unstoppable force of the young general and his now formidable, if still rag-tag, army and fixed his reputation as a hero both to his men and to the nation. It also ensured that the government in Paris could not supersede him, even when he openly refused to obey orders that he regarded as unsound.

Napoleon next outmanoeuvred Beaulieu's 30,000 men and by early June half the Austrian's troops were penned up in the powerful fortress of Mantua, which the French proceeded to besiege. Reinforcements from Germany enabled the Austrians to

attempt to relieve Mantua with 47,000 men under Marshal Würmser who, though defeated at Castiglione on 5 August, captured 179 French siege guns and managed to introduce reinforcements and supplies into the fortress to bolster its defence. Napoleon, however, struck again on 8 September, badly defeating Würmser at Bassano whence he retreated into Mantua with the 9,000 men left in his command. In a second attempt at relieving the city, Marshal Alvincy advanced with two columns down the Piave and Adige valleys, engaging Napoleon at Arcola in a three-day affair on 15–17 November that obliged him to withdraw. He tried again at Rivoli in early January 1797 but failed, and on 2 February, riddled with disease and exhausted through starvation, the garrison capitulated, bringing to an end all Austrian resistance in Italy and prompting them to request an armistice on 11 April. The Treaty of Campo Formio, concluded on 17 October, settled the terms without reference to Paris for instructions, thus demonstrating Napoleon's elevation from a mere soldier of the Republic to its diplomat, as well; the general, it seemed, entertained political ambitions.

Austria recognized French occupation of Belgium, Luxembourg and Habsburg territories on the west bank of the Rhine, abandoned her claims on Milan and Mantua and agreed that these cities and other Italian territory should become a French satellite, the Cisalpine Republic. Austria received Venice, but Campo Formio effectively put northern Italy under French control, converting the Adriatic into a French lake, providing access to the Ionian Sea, and thus rendering France the major power on the Continent, with Britain her only principal remaining rival.

With the conclusion of the Treaty of Campo Formio the priority for Napoleon – still only a general but now the most famous of them all – lay in defeating Britain, even if accomplishing this formidable objective remained unclear, for France alone did not possess sufficient naval assets for an invasion. Instead, now in a position to influence national strategy, Napoleon suggested striking at British interests in the Mediterranean by means of occupying Egypt, thereby threatening trade in the Levant and presenting the possibility of a descent on India. The Franco-Spanish alliance of 1796 having obliged

Above: At the battle of Arcola Napoleon leads troops across the bridge over the river Alpone, 15 November 1796. Although the assault failed, the episode played a prominent role in the creation of the Napoleonic legend. After a further two days' fighting the French captured the village and drove off the Austrians, making the fall of Mantua inevitable. (Author's collection)

Opposite: Napoleon in command of the ragged but highly motivated Armée de l'Italie, 1796. Through sheer force of character, stirring rhetoric and the promise of glory and booty, the young general transformed a hitherto ineffective body of poorly clothed and equipped troops into a first-rate fighting force. (Author's collection)

the Royal Navy to evacuate the Mediterranean apart from Gibraltar, the French fleet at Toulon could with relative impunity transport an army to Egypt. On 9 May Napoleon arrived in Toulon to supervise preparations, and with reinforcements from Italy and Corsica commanded an army of 31,000 men sailing in 300 transports and a large fleet. The expedition accepted Malta's surrender on 12 June and reached Alexandria on 1 July. Napoleon proceeded to fight two battles against the Mamelukes, after which he occupied Cairo and began to establish a new administration for the country, complete with hospitals, a postal service and a printing press, and issued instructions for the imposition of sanitary regulations in an effort to eradicate plague. He reopened blocked canals, introduced street lighting in Cairo, built windmills, and opened academic institutions with the aid of a body of savants who accompanied the expedition, including chemists, biologists and archaeologists.

Above: Napoleon at the battle of the Pyramids, 21 July 1798, in which he secured control of the Lower Nile by forming massive divisional squares and repelling a series of dashing yet uncoordinated Mameluke charges with disciplined musketry and artillery fire. Cairo fell the following day. (Author's collection)

Nevertheless, while victorious on land, Napoleon could not guarantee the safety of his fleet, which Lord Nelson annihilated in Aboukir Bay on 1 August, leaving the French Armée d'Orient stranded in Egypt and providing the Royal Navy with complete mastery of the Mediterranean. The British victory in fact accomplished much more: it reignited European resistance, and a second coalition sprang to life, including Austria and Russia, who promptly began operations in Germany, northern Italy and Switzerland. The Directory launched offensives on all fronts and failed everywhere. In distant Cairo, Napoleon suppressed a revolt in the city and marched north into

Palestine on news that the Turks were massing an army for the reconquest of Egypt. On 7 March he stormed Jaffa, but plague soon afflicted his army. He next advanced against the Turkish base at Acre, site of a Crusader fort that he besieged – but without the benefit of the heavy guns of his siege train which a Royal Navy squadron had captured at sea. He nevertheless invested the place between 18 March and 20 May, failing to take Acre despite numerous determined assaults. With losses of 2,200 dead, Napoleon retreated to Egypt where he drove into the sea a Turkish expedition of

8,000 troops that landed at Aboukir on 25 July.

Nevertheless, with the campaign clearly a failure and with French military prospects waning badly in Europe (apart from on the Swiss front), Napoleon decided to abandon his army and make his way back to France with a handful of his principal staff officers, many of them later becoming marshals under the Empire. On 9 October he landed at Fréjus, in southern France, precisely when the Directory stood on the brink of collapse owing to military failure, government financial cutbacks and the extension of conscription.

Above: Napoleon and his troops negotiate their way through the Alps into Italy via the St Bernard Pass during the campaign of 1800. The remarkable speed with which he moved his armies formed the hallmark of success in most of his campaigns. (Author's collection)

A coup was already in the making, and with the sudden appearance in Paris of Napoleon – hailed for his conquest of Egypt – the conspirators felt emboldened on 18 Brumaire (9 November 1799) to dissolve by force the legislative body known as the Council of Five Hundred, placing in their stead, by dubious election, three consuls, Napoleon amongst them. When, a month later, the new constitution proclaimed him First Consul, it laid the foundation for 15 years of absolute rule; the French Revolution was over and the Napoleonic era had begun.

Having achieved political pre-eminence, Napoleon now faced the problem of meeting the challenge posed by Austria, Britain and Russia – though Tsar Paul had grown disenchanted with his allies and was on the verge of leaving the alliance. Neither Britain nor Austria would accept peace proposals from France. The former retook Malta in 1800 and remained supreme at sea; the latter refused to concede her gains in northern Italy where Austrian forces had effectively reversed all the conquests made by Napoleon in the campaigns of 1796–97. This he set out to change by resuming the offensive in northern Italy while a second French army faced the Austrians on the upper Rhine. Napoleon decided to march an army across the Alps and confront General Melas, who on 5 April 1800 defeated General André Masséna's army and broke it in two, part of which took refuge in the fortress in Genoa, which the Austrians besieged by land and the Royal Navy bombarded by sea. For a change the Austrians' movements surprised Napoleon, whose 40,000 men did not reach the approaches of the Great St Bernard Pass until 14 May, with a further 25,000 men to enter Italy via two other passes. Masséna, his garrison reduced to its final rations and suffering from typhus, surrendered on 4 June; yet he had held a substantial Austrian force in check, by which time Napoleon had reached Milan. Within a week, General Jean Lannes defeated an Austrian detachment at Montebello and Napoleon had crossed the Po, interposing himself between Melas and his communication with Vienna.

Despite this brilliant strategic move, Napoleon proceeded to make a series of tactical blunders. With insufficient intelligence on the position or

Opposite: Napoleon exhorting his troops during an assault against the besieged town of Acre, the key engagement of his campaign in Syria, April 1799. With British assistance – including the capture at sea of the French siege train – the Turkish defenders successfully held the place, assisted by the outbreak of disease in the enemy camp. (Author's collection)

Napoleon at the battle of Marengo, 14 June 1800, fought during the second Italian campaign. By uncharacteristically dividing his forces while seeking out the Austrian main body, Napoleon exposed himself to an enveloping movement from which only the timely arrival of Desaix narrowly extricated both his army and his reputation. (Author's collection)

strength of the Austrians, he moved on the fortified city of Alessandria, detaching two corps north of the Po to secure his retreat. This left him with but 31,000, of whom over 5,000 he detached under General Desaix to cover a supposed threat from the direction of Genoa. Misreading Melas's intention, which in fact was to break out eastwards rather than retreat, Napoleon detached another division, of 3,500 men, on the morning of 14 June, to operate further north, leaving the main French army of only 22,000 faced by Melas's 28,500 men at Alessandria. Melas moved east out of Alessandria in three columns and began to overrun the French position at the village of Marengo, possession of which the Austrians secured by the afternoon, leaving the French sufficiently mauled as to retreat almost 8km (5 miles). But the battle was not quite decided; Desaix finally arrived with his division and attacked the enemy right, falling dead from his horse as his men drove the Austrians back.

The two sides concluded an armistice the following day and though Desaix and others accounted for the narrow French victory, Napoleon subverted reports and emerged with the lion's share of the glory. Five days after Marengo French forces in Germany beat the Austrians at Höchstadt and took Munich, though the Habsburgs were not prepared to accept disadvantageous terms until General Moreau decisively defeated them at Hohenlinden on 3 December. Peace was reached on 9 February 1801 at Lunéville, stripping Austria of her Italian territory beyond the Adige and obliging Vienna to recognize the French satellite states in the Low Countries, Switzerland and northern Italy. This settlement, like that reached at Campo Formio in 1797, left Britain almost entirely isolated. Still, she defeated the Danish fleet at Copenhagen in April 1801 and ousted the French from Egypt in September, leaving both sides to ponder the stalemate. With France victorious on land and the British similarly at sea, the two powers, anxious for a respite, agreed to terms at Amiens in March 1802.

THE HOUR OF DESTINY

As anticipated by both sides, who regarded Amiens as nothing more than a truce, the peace constituted merely an interlude in the long series of conflicts that had begun in 1792, known as the French Revolutionary Wars, and those that followed Amiens, with another brief interlude in 1814, until Waterloo in 1815, aptly styled the Napoleonic Wars. The renewed conflict, which began in May 1803, initially involved only Britain and France. As the dominant naval power, Britain naturally reverted to its time-honoured strategy of reimposing its blockade of the major French ports and preying on French commercial shipping. Napoleon, at the same time, resumed the construction of shallow-draught transports in preparation for a cross-Channel invasion of England by 160,000 troops. Over the subsequent months the main construction of vessels around Boulogne grew substantially, as did the concentration of troops established in camps there. The Emperor understood that so as to facilitate an invasion it was vital to distract a large proportion of the Royal Navy's ships in order to ensure that the Channel was clear for his highly vulnerable invasion craft. Napoleon, ignorant of naval strategy, failed to appreciate that the principles that applied to warfare on land did not necessarily apply to those at sea, devised many plans of varying complexity – to be dashed by Admiral Lord Nelson's spectacular victory at Trafalgar on 21 October 1805, putting paid to all further serious French attempts at invasion of the British Isles.

Britain was instrumental in organizing a third coalition, which came to fruition in April 1805 with the conclusion of an Anglo-Russian alliance, to which Austria acceded on 9 August. Accordingly, Napoleon broke up his invasion camp at Boulogne at the end of August and marched his forces, now designated the Grande Armée, to the Danube in order to confront the allied armies. At the same time, an Austrian army under General Mack, who had no knowledge that the French were moving east, invaded Bavaria, a French ally, on 2 September.

The Austrian commander-in-chief, Archduke Charles, meanwhile advanced into Italy to confront the French forces there under Marshal Masséna, while further east a Russian army under General Mikhail Kutusov slowly advanced through Poland to assist the Austrians in Moravia. The Austrians were shocked

Below left: Napoleon addressing troops of the Armée de l'Angleterre at the camp of Boulogne during preparations for a descent against southern England, c.1804. The greatest army of its day and thousands of shallow-draught boats were to be deployed for an expedition that never materialized. (Author's collection)

Below right: Napoleon receiving General Mack's surrender at Ulm, 20 October 1805, which marked the culmination of one of history's greatest strategic envelopments and the consequent elimination of an entire Austrian army from the campaign. (Author's collection)

to discover that Napoleon had made such remarkably rapid progress, crossing the Rhine on 26 September and reaching the Danube on 6 October. In the course of this march, the French had moved in a broad arc around Mack's army near Ulm, cutting his lines of communication and isolating him from reinforcement. After a feeble attempt to break through the cordon at Elchingen on 14 October, Mack surrendered his entire force of 27,000 men on 17 October, making the encirclement at Ulm one of history's greatest strategic manoeuvres.

With Mack's force neutralized, Napoleon advanced on and occupied Vienna, forcing the Russians back at Dürnstein on 11 November and Hollabrunn on 15–16 November. In Italy, Masséna was victorious at Caldiero, forcing Charles to retire back across the Alps, though detached formations from the principal French forces prevented him from linking up with the main Austro-Russian army, for which Napoleon set a trap. By moving north of the Austrian capital to expose his lines of communication, Napoleon tempted Kutusov to sever these lines. The ploy worked, drawing the Russians and Austrians towards Napoleon in what appeared to them a strong position.

Austerlitz, 2 December 1805

With both armies in close proximity to one another, Napoleon had to ensure that the Russians remained and fought – a prospect that looked favourable since with the presence of the Austrians the strategic advantage appeared now to lie with the Allies. With his army now deep in the heart of Europe, it was critical that Napoleon achieve a decisive victory, for with the Prussians neutral yet preparing to join the Third Coalition the Allies stood to crush him through overwhelming numbers alone. Napoleon therefore faced four prospects: first, if Kutusov chose to beat a hasty retreat and successfully elude the French, Napoleon would be denied the decisive battle he sought, and would have no choice but to withdraw, with the Allies left intact. Nor, secondly, would a drawn battle achieve his ends, for again the Allies would remain as a potential force. Thirdly, if Napoleon was obliged to confront a

Napoleon and his headquarters staff

The Emperor (**1**) is shown in the basic style of dress he favoured in the period from Austerlitz to Waterloo (1805–15): a black leather, unadorned cocked hat bearing a simple cockade and the green jacket of a mounted Chasseur of the Imperial Guard. Often sporting the uniform of a hussar, Imperial aides-de-camp, as shown here, c.1804 (**2**) delivered the Emperor's orders and conveyed messages to him from corps and divisional commanders in the field. Behind Napoleon sits a colonel on the Staff (**3**), c.1809. A marshal of the Empire, c.1805 (**4**), of whom the Emperor created 26 between 1804 and 1815, led one or more corps. Roustam (**5**), the Emperor's personal Mameluke servant – a legacy of the Egyptian campaign of 1798 – faithfully served his master until Napoleon's abdication in 1814. Personal servants of the Imperial household (**6**) managed the Emperor's personal effects while his superbly reliable chief of staff, Marshal Berthier (**7**), ensured that orders were conveyed and discharged accurately and efficiently. Grenadiers of the Imperial Guard stand in formation to the rear – the Emperor's ultimate reserve.

Marshal Bernadotte, commander of I Corps at Austerlitz. His conduct there disappointed the Emperor, who the following year blamed Bernadotte for failing to reach the battlefield at Jena and later accused him of dithering at Wagram in the campaign of 1809. The marshal eventually left Napoleon's service and became king of Sweden, serving in the campaigns of 1813–14 against his former master. (Author's collection)

numerically superior enemy force on ground of its own choosing, he would suffer from a serious tactical disadvantage. This left a fourth – and the most viable – option: somehow to persuade the Allies to attack him at a time and place of his choosing. This was the strategy Napoleon pursued.

Such a course naturally depended on the Russians accepting the bait Napoleon intended to offer, which was to persuade them that they outnumbered him by a factor of two to one and that, suddenly made aware of his predicament, he was at a loss to respond. As such, Napoleon spent the next ten days pursuing a campaign of bluff and espionage. General Savary was sent to Tsar Alexander's headquarters at Olmütz to assess the Russians' mood and sound them out on the question of a negotiated peace, which he disingenuously suggested the Emperor, concerned about his isolated position, was keen to conclude. While the Grande Armée sat idle, suggesting indecisiveness, Napoleon sent out aides to bring in the corps of marshals Davout and Bernadotte and all other formations for the coming battle. At the same time, the Emperor, reviewing the campaigns conducted in the area by Frederick the Great in the mid-18th century and copiously studying maps supplied by his cartographical department, personally rode over the countryside between Brünn and Olmütz, looking for favourable ground on which to confront the Austro-Russian armies. After careful thought he chose a position between Brünn and the small village of Austerlitz, about 21km (13 miles) to the east.

The Allies decided on an offensive battle for the following day, using a plan to fix Napoleon in front of the commanding Pratzen Heights, so leaving him with the impression that he faced the threat of a frontal attack there by numerically superior opponents. In reality, 55,000 men of a total force of 89,000 would move southwards to strike the French right flank between Telnitz and Sokolnitz. Having crossed the Goldbach Brook and penetrated French defences, the Russian general Buxhöwden's spearhead would extend outwards to cut the French lines of communication with Vienna and encircle the French army from the rear. In the meanwhile, the remainder of the Russian line would hold the line on the right under General Bagration, while the Russian Imperial Guard – a mere 10,000 men, but an elite formation – would hold the Pratzen Heights in the centre under Grand Duke Constantine, the Tsar's brother.

The battlefield extended over a small area stretching 26km (16 miles) from Brünn to Austerlitz. The actual length of the front measured, from north to south, less than 16km (10 miles). The Goldbach Brook and its tributary, the Bosenitz, which crossed the field, constituted marshy streams. There were no features of striking elevation save for the Pratzen Heights, but even these rose only 98m (320ft) above sea level. On the northern extreme of the field were wooded hills, making an outflanking movement here impossible to both sides. Between the Heights and the main road extending east–west between Brunn and Olmütz stood a mound known as the Santon, 200m (660ft) in height on the French side of the lines. The Pratzen Heights stood south of the main road, in Russian possession, and provided a commanding

Napoleon inspecting troops at the camp of the Grande Armée on the eve of Austerlitz. The Emperor routinely walked among his troops prior to battle, speaking of past victories, chatting with soldiers and exhorting them to success with grandiose speeches promising immortal glory. (Author's collection)

view of the battlefield. To the south lay the villages of Kobelnitz, Sokolnitz and Telnitz; the Goldbach meandered through boggy water meadows in which lay a number of small shallow lakes, all frozen over.

Napoleon's basic plan was to encourage the Allies to outflank him to the south. By doing so, they would be risking exposing their own flank on the Pratzen Heights as they executed this manoeuvre. To encourage them to take this risk the Emperor would abandon the Heights, feigning nervousness. Key to his stratagem was the Santon, which was to be preserved in French hands at all costs, and whose fortification by the French prior to the battle strongly suggested to his opponents that Napoleon intended to remain static and await an Allied frontal attack at the northern end of his line. By weakening his defences between Kobelnitz and Telnitz Napoleon deliberately sought to entice an Allied attack there. But the Emperor had no intention of remaining on the defensive, for he would form up behind the centre of the line 30,000 men from Marshal Soult's corps, supported by Bernadotte's corps and the vaunted Imperial Guard. None of these formations would be observable to the enemy. As soon as the Allies had begun their flanking march and removed most of their troops from the Pratzen Heights, Soult would assault them, seizing a position previously deemed virtually unassailable and therefore the point at which an attack would least be expected. If he succeeded, Napoleon would then encircle the enemy from the rear, pushing back the enemy's formations against the Menitz and Satschan ponds. Having destroyed the Austro-Russian main body, he would then shift northwards to attack Bagration's force, which marshals Murat and Lannes would have engaged on the left part of the line. By nightfall on 1 December the Emperor had shifted his troops in accordance with the movements of the enemy southwards, as he desired.

At dawn on 2 December, Napoleon mustered 73,000 men with 139 cannon against 89,000 Allied troops, of whom about 16,000 were Russians and the remaining Austrian, together with 278 guns. Three Russian columns began to descend the Pratzen Heights moving southwards under Buxhöwden.

Battle of Austerlitz, 2 December 1805, situation about 1000hrs

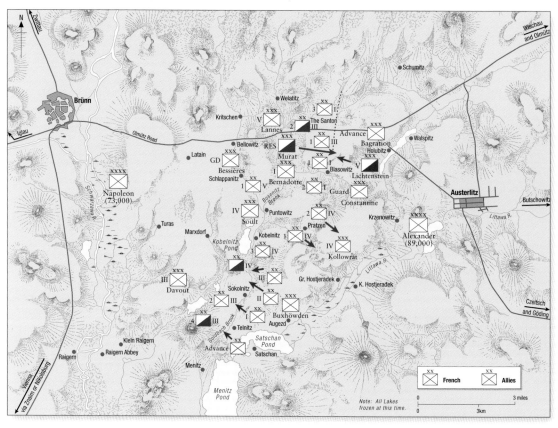

In command of the advance guard, opposite Telnitz, was General Keinmeyer, with 6,800 men, mostly Austrians. Following them were the Russian general Dokhturov with 13,700 men and Langeron, a French émigré in the Tsar's service, with 11,700. Further to the north came 7,800 under General Prszebyszewski, and finally Kollowrath and Miloradovich, Austrian and Russian generals, respectively, with 23,000. Thick fog obscured the ground and many Austrian and Russian units became intermingled, with confusion reigning all round. When, owing to his misreading of a map, Prince John of Lichtenstein accidentally deployed his cavalry 5km (3 miles) further south than intended, the delay in returning them to their proper position in turn set back Buxhöwden's planned assault by an hour.

The battle began at about 0700hrs when the Austrians under Kienmeyer struck the end of the French line at Telnitz. In defence in the area between Telnitz and Kobelnitz stood the 6,000 men of General Legrand's division, not yet supported by Davout's III Corps, which was en route. In the meantime, 55,000 men under Buxhöwden were approaching. Legrand's men managed to hold off the piecemeal Allied advance, but at 0800hrs Dokhturov's column made contact and Keinmeyer launched a cavalry charge. The French line held for a while, but against overwhelming numerical superiority it could not resist indefinitely.

The French were under even greater pressure further north, where Langeron and Prszebyszewski, leading 20,000 men, were on the attack. Nevertheless, they were also delayed by an hour because of Lichtenstein's earlier mistake, and more time was lost when the Russians became congested during the crossing of the Goldbach. At that moment General Friant's vanguard of III Corps was moving north for Kobelnitz, until a messenger appeared bearing urgent orders to proceed with all possible haste to the Telnitz–Sokolnitz sector. Friant duly arrived, but Langeron massed 30 guns and tore a hole through the French line, and with the Allies pressing forward with greatly superior numbers, by 0900hrs Dokhturov had taken Telnitz, Langeron held Sokolnitz, and Prszebyszewski had seized Sokolnitz Castle. This now left the bridgeheads across the Goldbach in Allied hands and there appeared little to stop them moving into the plain opposite.

Napoleon meanwhile stood at his command post on high ground by Bellowitz, where he considered the position of the Pratzen Heights, 5km (3 miles) to the south-east, an area shrouded in mist like so much of the battlefield. It was vital to Napoleon's plans that the mist not dissipate too early, for it cloaked Soult's corps, deployed in the Bosenitz Valley, and the Emperor did not want the Allies to be aware of its presence as it awaited the right moment for attack. Yet nor did he want the mist to linger too long, for then he would be unable to determine when Buxhöwden had evacuated the Pratzen Heights, so preventing him from timing his attack properly.

But at about 0800hrs the sun began to appear through the mist, slowly clearing it away and revealing large numbers of Allied troops streaming southwards down the Pratzen Heights. It was nearing the time when Soult's

Above left: Marshal Nicolas Soult. As commander of IV Corps he led the attack on the Pratzen Heights at Austerlitz. Serving with distinction at Jena in 1806 and at Eylau in 1807, Soult later led a corps in Spain before becoming commander of all French forces there in 1813. (Author's collection)

Above right: Marshal Murat leading a charge during the Austerlitz campaign. The most flamboyant of Napoleon's subordinates, Murat epitomized the brash indifference to death so prevalent amongst cavalry officers of the day. (Author's collection)

corps, still shrouded in mist and obscured by campfire smoke, would be launched. As soon as Napoleon observed that Kollowrath and Miloradovich had vacated the plateau, he issued the critical order, and 17,000 men of Soult's corps began their swift march in *ordre mixte*, causing the Tsar and his entourage at Russian headquarters to look with astonishment upon two divisions suddenly appearing out of the mist. On the right, St Hilaire's division swept into the village of Pratzen and on to the knoll of Pratzeberg with no resistance. On the left, General Vandamme's division fought hard for half an hour through Girzikovitz and beyond it, seizing the Stari Vinbrady knoll, such that by 0930hrs Soult held indisputable possession of the Pratzen Heights, with the Allies routed and moving rapidly in disarray towards Austerlitz.

The surprise of Soult's appearance and the small numbers of Allied troops on the Pratzen had assured French success there. Kutusov ordered Miloradovich to reverse the front of his rear columns, but only a few were able to do so, while he told Constantine that the Imperial Guard, held in reserve back at Krzenowitz, might have to be committed. Napoleon, appreciating the extent of his success in the centre, ordered Soult to consolidate his hold on the Pratzen Heights in expectation that the Allies would counterattack. Bernadotte's I Corps, at the same time, was sent forwards in support, capturing Blasowitz to the left of Soult's position until two battalions of the Russian Imperial Guard drove him out.

While hitherto the northern sector of the battle had remained quiet, this changed at about 1000hrs, during a brief respite in the centre. Murat and Lannes had orders to keep Bagration out of the main battle. When the Russian Imperial Guard took Blasowitz, Lannes moved up two divisions for the purpose of pushing Bagration towards the north and enabling Murat to deploy his cavalry in the widening gap thus created in the Allied front. At about this time Prince Lichtenstein arrived on Bagration's flank and threw in some of the Russian Guard cavalry against General Caffarelli's division, later backed by a steadily escalating cavalry action. This proved of no avail, however, for French infantry deployed in square, supported by cavalry charging from the flank, badly repulsed the Allied horsemen, enabling Caffarelli to continue his advance. Bagration duly brought forward 40 guns, against which accurate French counterbattery fire replied with considerable effect.

This great artillery duel finished at around 1030hrs, when infantry on both sides resumed the advance. At the northern extreme of the line, Bagration sought to outflank Lannes with a spirited attack on the Santon, but as this was vital to Napoleon's position, the Emperor was determined to defend it at all costs. Bagration's troops took the hamlet of Bosenitz and reached a point 400m (437 yards) beyond, but a combination of all arms halted their attack, while at the other end of the line, infantry under Lannes, with cavalry in support, retook Bosenitz with the bayonet and began to move beyond the village. Meanwhile, Lichtenstein, determined to bring a halt to Caffarelli's advance, launched a strong cavalry attack comprising nearly 6,000 men. The French infantry repulsed three such attacks in succession before Murat, though outnumbered nearly two to one, threw into the fray a body of heavy cavalry which, in this the second and larger cavalry action of the day, broke the Allied horsemen and forced them back.

Thus, by noon, Lannes and Murat had held off the Allied offensive on the northern sector, having inflicted 4,000 casualties and captured the same number in prisoners. Napoleon's principal achievement had been in excluding Bagration from the decisive fighting taking place in the centre. Nevertheless, the Russian commander's force remained largely intact and he continued to block the road to Olmütz, the route that the Emperor proposed to use in his final, devastating blow.

On the other end of the line, the French remained heavily outnumbered and scarcely able to resist the Allied onslaught. Still, Davout's III Corps, the finest and most efficient corps in the Grande Armée, was en route – having just completed a stunning 140km (87-mile) forced march – coming under heavy fire before crossing the Goldbach and recapturing Telnitz from Keinmeyer's Austrians, only to lose it again at 0900hrs. At Solkonitz the fighting was even worse, with Langeron's Russians exchanging possession several times despite a grave disparity in numbers: 8,000 French infantry and 2,800 cavalry against 35,000 Allies, whose forces became jammed on the bridges whilst trying to cross the Goldbach. Around 1000hrs, concerned at the fragility of Davout's position, Napoleon ordered grenadiers from Oudinot's reserve to proceed south and reinforce the line. Still, the Allies were now beginning to perceive their own predicament, for Soult's occupation of the Pratzen Heights placed him behind the bulk of Austro-Russian forces.

There the Allied counterattack now began, causing serious problems for Soult, with St Hilaire's division bearing the brunt of the fighting and Russian forces attacking from three sides, for there were rather more enemy infantry left on the south-east slopes of the Heights than Napoleon had realized. No sooner was St Hilaire about to be overrun when, instead of executing a contemplated withdrawal, he launched a bayonet attack supported by a battery of reserve artillery. By his extraordinary decision, St Hilaire's men repulsed the Austrians and Russians, with many of the latter dying where they stood as the round shot tore through their ranks.

By midday, with the air now growing bitterly cold and the battlefield obscured with smoke, there was still much fighting ahead, but Bagration had been kept isolated from the main effort in the centre, where the French had successfully held off the Allied counterattacks. Soult therefore held most of the Pratzen Heights while to the right Davout had so far managed – though only barely – to keep back the Allies' attempt to encircle him.

Also around noon, Napoleon had established the new site of his head-quarters on the Pratzen Heights. Shortly

Russian infantry and artillery crashing through the ice during their frenzied retreat at Austerlitz. Napoleon exaggerated their losses in his bulletin, but the episode reflected the disastrous nature of the Allied defeat. (Author's collection)

thereafter he was ready to begin the decisive stage of the action, and ordered Soult's corps to adjust its direction and threaten the flank and rear of Buxhöwden's formations. Bernadotte's I Corps, shifted away from the fighting with Bagration, was ordered to replace Soult's corps on the Pratzen and drive the remaining Allied troops in the centre back in the direction of Austerlitz. At the same time, Davout was to assume the offensive against Buxhöwden. In the meantime, Murat and Lannes, to the north, had yet to receive new orders. It remained only for Napoleon to succeed in the centre, where Constantine's corps of the Russian Imperial Guard now stood. Vandamme managed to withstand an infantry attack, after which the Guard retired in good order towards Krzenowitz. Napoleon then ordered Vandamme to wheel to the right in pursuit, with Bernadotte's corps following slowly behind.

Constantine now decided the time was ripe to throw in the cavalry of the Russian Imperial Guard. These thundered forward, catching two of Vandamme's regiments by total surprise, routing their opponents and capturing an eagle, whereupon Napoleon sent in Marshal Bessières with his own Guard cavalry to stabilize the deteriorating situation. Bernadotte's infantry were now beginning to appear on the Heights, as well. The combination proved too much, and the Russian elite cavalry were driven away with heavy casualties and their commander taken prisoner. The Allied centre had collapsed.

Napoleon now perceived that the moment had come for a general offensive, and shortly after 1330hrs ordered 25,000 men to move southwards off the Pratzen Heights and destroy Buxhöwden. The pace of battle now accelerated rapidly. Vandamme, on the extreme left of the net cast by the Emperor, reached Augezd in only an hour, thus creating a barrier to any escape to the east, except across the river Littawa, a feature lined with virtually impassable bogs. Beside Vandamme came St Hilaire, moving rapidly down the east bank of the Goldbach, supported by Oudinot's grenadier division. On the opposite side of the Goldbach lay Friant who, though his division had lost 2,000 casualties in the morning's combat, was in the midst of retaking Sokolnitz, by now choked with dead and wounded. With Davout also engaged, the net was fast closing on the Allies from three sides, forcing Buxhöwden towards the Satschen and Menitz ponds on the fourth side.

Napoleon at Austerlitz

In the foreground a cuirassier displays captured Russian colours while guarding an officer of Hungarian grenadiers and a Russian general. Shortly after 0800hrs the fog lifted from the Pratzen Heights to reveal the last of the Allied troops departing that position and moving south. Here, an aide-de-camp hands the Emperor a message confirming the fact, which prompts him shortly thereafter to order Soult, whose troops are concealed by mist at the foot of the slopes, to occupy the Heights. Two divisions, under Vandamme and St Hilaire, respectively, advanced briskly, surprising and overwhelming with their superior numbers those defenders still occupying the Heights, marking the beginning of an enveloping movement that finished with a crushing French victory widely regarded as Napoleon's most impressive tactical success.

Somehow, in the confusion, Kutusov's order to retreat, issued three hours earlier, had failed to reach the various corps commanders. Now the retreat was becoming a rout, leaving many trapped, like Prszebyszewski's men in Sokolnitz, where after eight hours' fighting and finding themselves assailed on three sides with no hope of support, they had no alternative but to surrender. Dokhturov, with 5,000 men pinned against the ponds, counterattacked, while Cossacks scouted for a route of escape between the ponds. But the Russians could not withstand the French onslaught, and while Kienmeyer had managed to identify a space between the ponds for his Austrians, who had fought a splendid withdrawal, many of the fleeing Russians failed to locate it and instead proceeded across the ice-covered ponds – a fatal decision. Even under the weight of fleeing cavalry and artillery teams the ice continued to bear up, but when Napoleon ordered an artillery bombardment of the position the ice began to crack, plunging horses, guns and infantry into the freezing waters.

Perhaps 2,000 men drowned and about 40 guns were lost, with another 2,000 prisoners rescued by Napoleon's pursuing forces. But even such relatively small numbers only served to underline the dreadful nature of the Allied defeat, which left large numbers of prisoners in French hands, including Buxhöwden. Only Bagration's corps amongst the rest of Allied formations remained more or less intact, not least owing to the fact that, having by midday utterly neutralized him, Murat, Lannes and Bernadotte took no further initiative, and by 1500hrs Bagration had begun to withdraw in an orderly fashion. Napoleon had not issued fresh instructions to his subordinates on the northern flank, but rather had assumed that once Soult had broken through the centre and begun the enveloping movement to the right, Murat would follow suit with his own manoeuvre around Bagration's rear. By 1630hrs, as the firing had all but ceased along the northern sector and darkness was descending over the battlefield, Bagration had removed his corps beyond Murat's clutches, even while faced by Bernadotte's slow-moving I Corps, which did nothing to impede the Russian commander's withdrawal. Thus, decisive though Austerlitz indisputably was, Bagration's escape robbed Napoleon of the truly overwhelming success he had sought.

The losses sustained at Austerlitz are disputed, but French dead probably numbered only 2,000, with about 7,000 wounded and approximately 600 taken prisoner. Because of the inaction of Napoleon's Imperial Guard and most of Bernadotte's corps, the actual number of fighting Frenchmen numbered about 45,000, as opposed to about 90,000 Austrians and Russians, rendering their defeat all the more substantial. Allied losses are reckoned at about 15,000 killed and wounded, all but 4,000 of these being Russian. A further 12,000 troops fell into French hands, for a total of 27,000 lost to the Allies, plus 180 guns and 45 flags, as against almost 10,000 for the French. The Tsar retreated back to Russia via Hungary, leaving the Emperor Francis to negotiate terms with Napoleon.

Austerlitz stands as one of the greatest victories in military history. Napoleon's prowess and the effectiveness of the Grande Armée as a fighting force reached its apogee there, and it constituted the battle of which the Emperor himself was most proud. In 20 days he had marched his army from Boulogne to the Rhine; in two months it had entered the Austrian capital; and three days later he had destroyed the Third Coalition. Napoleon had gambled supremely in the campaign of 1805, and generally gambled correctly. If any single factor contributed to success it was speed, which enabled him to encircle Mack before the Russians could come to his aid. But luck also played a part in

Napoleon meeting Emperor Francis II of Austria after the battle of Austerlitz. The Habsburgs' territorial concessions in northern Italy and along the Adriatic, in addition to their abrogation of influence in the German states, played a pivotal role in the rapid expansion of the Napoleonic Empire. (Author's collection)

his success, for had archdukes Charles and John combined forces the outcome of the campaign might have been very different. On 26 December Napoleon and Francis concluded a treaty of peace at Pressburg, where the latter agreed to cede extensive German and Italian territory to France, so compounding to the Empire those gains made by the Republic.

From Austerlitz to Borodino, 1805–12

Although Austria withdrew from the coalition after Austerlitz, Britain and Russia remained at war with France. The Fourth Coalition came into being in the autumn of 1806 after a breakdown in Franco-Prussian relations. After the Allied disaster at Austerlitz Prussia chose to maintain her neutrality – in hindsight a grave strategic error on its part – but with the growing influence of France in German affairs it threw in its lot and declared war in the autumn of 1806.

The Grande Armée, situated in north-east Bavaria, invaded Prussia, defeating the Prussian Army at Jena and Auerstädt on 14 October. The destruction of Prussia's main army effectively spelled the end of resistance. Berlin itself fell on 24 October, and the last major force to hold out, near Lübeck, surrendered a month later.

With Prussia knocked out of the war, Napoleon sought out the Russian army under General Bennigsen, with the first encounter taking place on 26 December at Pultusk, where the Russians were bruised but nothing more. The rival armies went into winter quarters in January 1807 amid bitterly cold temperatures, but the campaign resumed the following month, when Bennigsen began to move and Napoleon went in pursuit. Though outnumbered and caught in a blizzard, Napoleon reached the Russians at Eylau where on 8 February the two sides inflicted severe losses on one another with no decisive result. Bennigsen withdrew, but with appalling losses and atrocious weather, Napoleon declined to follow. Both sides returned to winter quarters to recover from the carnage, with the renewal of hostilities planned for the spring.

Bennigsen and Napoleon each planned to assume the offensive, but when the former advanced first, the Emperor stopped him at Heilsberg on 10 June. Four days later the decisive encounter of the campaign took place at Friedland, where Bennigsen foolishly placed his army with the river Alle at his back. The Russians resisted Napoleon's attacks with magnificent stoicism, eventually collapsing. With no route of escape, the campaign was over. Tsar Alexander, his army in tatters, and accompanied by Frederick William of Prussia, requested a conference to discuss peace. The three sovereigns concluded the Treaty of Tilsit between 7 and 9 July, putting the seal on Napoleonic control of Europe from the Vistula in the east to the Atlantic in the west; from Danzig in the north to Trieste in the south.

With Russia and Prussia knocked out of the war, only Britain remained to face France, now at the height of its power. To combat his last remaining adversary, Napoleon had already issued his Berlin and Milan Decrees, inaugurating the Continental System, by which he sought to impose an embargo on the importation of British goods to mainland ports and the exportation

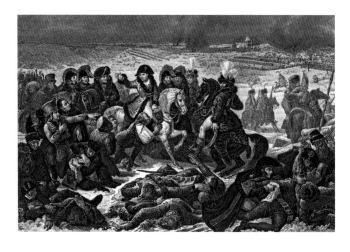

of Continental goods to Britain in an effort to strangle its economy.

After the Treaty of Tilsit and the introduction of the Continental System, only Portugal continued to defy the ban by accepting British imports. In an effort to close this final avenue of trade, Napoleon sent troops through Spain to Portugal, taking advantage of the opportunity to impose his will on the Spanish, as well. General Andoche Junot took Lisbon without a fight, but the French occupation of Spain was never fated to go smoothly; on 2 May 1808 the populace of Madrid rose up in revolt, and the spirit of resistance soon spread throughout the country, where guerrilla bands began to spring up and prey on French detachments and isolated outposts. The regular Spanish armies fought a number of pitched battles against the French, but they were generally defeated, sometimes disastrously.

The war in the Peninsula took on an entirely different character from August 1808, when a British expeditionary force cleared French troops from Portugal, with further reinforcements arriving under General Sir John Moore offering an opportunity for an offensive into Spain. Napoleon himself crossed the Pyrenees and drove Moore back towards Corunna, where, despite winning a victory, the British were forced out of the country.

Above: Napoleon at the battle of Wagram. The campaign against Austria in 1809 marked a transition from the earlier years of spectacular enveloping movements, decisive victories and relentless pursuits. (Author's collection)

Having defeated his enemies in Spain – though a small British force remained in Portugal – Napoleon went on the offensive against Austria and, having taken Vienna and suffered a setback at the battle of Aspern-Essling, defeated the Austrians at the battle of Wagram on 21–22 May. Austria could no longer carry on the war: Vienna was under enemy occupation, the main army had been beaten, though not destroyed, and Russia had not joined the campaign as Austria had hoped. Francis duly sued for peace and by the Treaty of Schönbrunn relinquished large portions of his empire to France and its allies and promised to adhere to the Continental System.

However, over the following years relations with Russia deteriorated to the point where war broke out again in 1812. Napoleon, gathering a massive army of unprecedented size and composed of every nationality from his empire, pushed across the Niemen River with over half a million men on 22 June 1812. The two main Russian armies, one under General Barclay de Tolly and the other under Bagration, found themselves unable to resist a force of this size, and withdrew eastwards, uniting at Smolensk on 3 August. Unable to outflank his opponents, Napoleon chose to engage them first on the 17th, where he took Smolensk by storm, and again at Valutino two days later, where he scored a minor success, the Russians simply withdrawing deeper into the interior and obliging the French to extend their increasingly vulnerable lines of communication even further.

Below: Napoleon accepting the surrender of Madrid from the city's deputies, December 1808. (Author's collection)

Left: Napoleon at the river Danube during the 1809 campaign against Austria. After inflicting a series of minor defeats on his opponents in late April, the Emperor moved his forces along the southern bank of the river and took Vienna on 13 May, only to be checked a week later at Aspern-Essling when trying to cross to the northern side. (Author's collection)

Right: Napoleon at the passage of the river Niemen by the Grande Armée, 22 June 1812. The immense size of his forces demanded that, in violation of all the sound principles that governed mobility and efficient logistics, an immense baggage and supply train accompanied the army, rendering it exceedingly ponderous, heavily dependent on supply depots and its extended lines of communication exceptionally vulnerable. (Author's collection)

Kutusov, who replaced Barclay de Tolly as commander-in-chief of all Russian forces, at last decided to make a stand before Moscow, choosing a position around the village of Borodino, about 115km (71 miles) to the west of the city.

Borodino, 7 September 1812

Russian dispositions were based on a largely static defence, with their right under the command of Barclay de Tolly and their left under Bagration. Kutusov established his line on a ridge that looked down on the Semenovskaya creek, with his forces straddling Borodino in his centre. His right wing faced north, running parallel to the south bank of the shallow Kalatsha River as far as its confluence with the Moskva; his left, facing west, extended southwards from the formidable Rayevsky (or 'Great') Redoubt (mounting 18 pieces of artillery and protected to the front by 'wolf pits' dug the previous day) through the ruined village of Semenovskaya, then past three arrow-shaped earthworks known as *flèches* to the village of Utitsa, which sat atop a knoll on the Old Post Road, beside which stood thick woodland. Heavy brush and trees, not least the Utitsa woods, covered much of Kutusov's position. Large bodies of Cossacks, unreliable against formed bodies of troops but effective in harassment, scouting and post-battle pursuit, protected both flanks. Finally, light infantry extended along the entire front. Several brooks intersected the area; these, and the knoll, woods and ridges at various points along a position measuring only 8km (5 miles) long, left exceptionally little room for manoeuvre; conversely, there would be plenty of opportunity for massed artillery to wreak havoc amidst the tightly packed formations on both sides.

The field fortifications along the main Russian line, though rapidly constructed, were by no means unimpressive. Earthwork structures manned with artillery stood around Borodino, near Utitsa and on the right flank covering the fords of the Kalatsha River. The two most formidable, however, were the Rayevsky Redoubt and the *flèches* built by Bagration. The Russian reserves were kept close to the front line, a great mistake as they were to make an ideal target for massed French artillery.

With their left anchored on woods and their centre strongly fortified, the Russians probably expected Napoleon to turn their right, and hence the relatively stronger dispositions around Gorki, the site of Kutusov's headquarters.

Napoleon, however, decided against making his main thrust against the Russian right on account of the high banks of the Kalatsha. He also rejected Davout's proposal for a wide, sweeping manoeuvre to the south with 40,000 men, intended to outflank Kutusov's left – a plan fraught with potential difficulties and yet, if successful, possibly decisive. Having insufficient troops to both pin the enemy and execute a wide turn around Kutusov's flank may have dissuaded Napoleon from adopting the plan. Whatever the reason, the Emperor, suffering from a heavy cold, failed to display his usual energy and opted for a simple strategy: a massive frontal assault on the Russian centre and centre-left. Specifically, he would direct the main thrust against the area between Borodino to the north and the *flêches* to the south, with Prince Poniatowski's V Corps, on its own, attempting a small flanking movement against the enemy left. This was perhaps the least imaginative and potentially costliest method of defeating the Russians, known for the exceptional steadfastness with which they defended ground.

The French were in position by 0500hrs on 7 September, but at sunrise, through some oversight made the previous day, the batteries were found to have been constructed out of range of the Russian line. Once they had been repositioned to within 1,200m (1,300 yards) of the enemy it was precisely 0600hrs, at which time 100 guns opened a massive bombardment against Bagration's positions. The French enjoyed some initial success, as IV Corps (mostly Italians) under Prince Eugène de Beauharnais, operating on the left of the attack, captured Borodino in a rapid assault. Barclay de Tolly's counterattack managed to retake the village, but finding the place untenable, the general ordered his troops to withdraw across the Kalatsha and burn the bridge behind them.

Meanwhile, two divisions under Davout reached Semenovskaya further south, while at 0630hrs the French made their first assault on the *flêches*, briefly taking one of them. Having lost heavily from artillery fire in the process, however, they soon retreated before a Russian counterattack with bayonets. Davout had his horse shot from under him and was carried off the field semi-conscious. On the extreme right, Poniatowski began his efforts at turning the Russian left. He succeeded in capturing Utitsa and part of the woods to the north of the village, aided by the transfer of some of the Russian troops in this sector to the area around the hard-pressed *flêches*. General Alexander Tuchkov was killed in the seesaw battle around Utitsa, where the Poles, despite gallant efforts, found themselves unable to achieve a breakthrough. Kutusov reacted accordingly, shifting large numbers of reserves from his as-yet unengaged right wing in order to reinforce his centre and left.

Back at the *flêches*, a Russian grenadier division struggled against overwhelming numbers of attackers

Marshal Murat. Commander of Napoleon's cavalry and of the advance guard during the invasion of Russia, he performed with his usual panache at Smolensk and Borodino and was the first officer to enter Moscow. When the Emperor left for Paris in December, command devolved upon Murat. (Author's collection)

Battle of Borodino, 7 September 1812, situation about 0930hrs

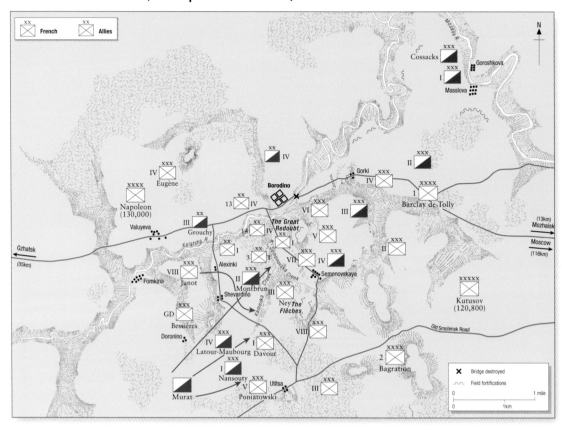

until virtually annihilated; like so many Russian units, especially those regiments within easy range of Napoleon's plentiful artillery, they died where they stood, stubbornly refusing to yield ground. The French eventually took two *flêches*, but before the third could be captured Bagration introduced reinforcements into the fray, which in turn drew in tens of thousands of French troops in a fierce hand-to-hand struggle that involved hundreds of pieces of artillery on both sides. The *flêches* changed hands several times, and in the course of the fighting Bagration fell wounded, struck in the leg – a wound from which he would die 17 days later. From Bagration command passed first to General Peter Konovnitsyn and then to Dokhturov, and after five hours' savage fighting the Russians finally withdrew from the *flêches*, the place littered with the fallen.

Further north, Eugène and his corps crossed the Kalatsha in the direction of the Rayevsky Redoubt but were halted with severe losses. Similarly, Davout's I Corps, confronting the corps of generals Rayevsky, Borodin and Baggovut and supported by part of Ney's command and all of Junot's corps, could not make further headway. After four hours' fighting, by 1000hrs the battle had degenerated into a massive contest of attrition, with rapidly growing casualties on both sides. Napoleon had long since committed practically all his formations save for the Imperial Guard and the cavalry held in reserve.

Subordinates appealed in vain to the Emperor to commit the Guard to take advantage of the fall of the *flêches*, but Napoleon refused, perhaps conscious of the fact that it might be needed at a more critical time.

By noon the Russians had partly given way in the centre, but they continued to hold the line in other sectors of the field. Kutusov redeployed General Osterman-Tolstoy's IV Corps from the right wing in order to bolster the centre and left, while 12,000 Cossacks and regular cavalry under generals Platov and Uvarov crossed the Kalatsha to counterattack Borodino, obliging the French to postpone their planned massive onslaught against the Great Redoubt. Meanwhile, by 1400hrs Eugène had recrossed the Kalatsha to the north bank in order to bolster the troops under attack by Russian cavalry and to ready his three divisions for the great assault. An earlier attack on the redoubt had been repulsed, leaving the French 30th Line virtually destroyed and the commander of the Russian reserve artillery, Kutaisov, dead. Grouchy's III Cavalry Corps was sent to cut up the Russian infantry in the area, but when they formed square his enterprise failed. After the cavalry returned to friendly lines the artillery bombardment was redoubled, killing thousands in the tightly packed Russian ranks, though the Rayevsky Redoubt remained in Russian possession.

At the same time, on Napoleon's extreme right, Poniatowski had made little further progress around Utitsa. Having the advantage of woods and broken ground, the defenders held their positions tenaciously, despite the appearance of French reinforcements under Junot.

With no possibility of a breakthrough on either wing, the French could only clinch victory in the centre. Situated in the Russian line between the Rayevsky

Left: Prince Eugène de Beauharnais, the son of Joséphine de Beauharnais by her first marriage and thus Napoleon's stepson. He commanded Italian troops against the Russians in 1812. (Author's collection)

Right: Prince Poniatowski, a national hero of his native Poland, commanded V Corps of the Grande Armée in Russia, where his troops fought with distinction at Smolensk and Borodino, largely motivated by hatred of the Russians and a desire for a resurrected Polish state. (Author's collection)

Marshal Davout. Considered one of Napoleon's finest marshals, he commanded III Corps at Austerlitz, defeated the Prussians decisively at Auerstädt in 1806 and served with distinction in the campaigns of 1807 and 1809. He was seriously wounded at Borodino, but survived to lead the rearguard during the retreat from Moscow. (Author's collection)

Redoubt and the *flêches*, Semenovskaya, already burned and virtually demolished, was now utterly destroyed by French artillery fire before two of Ney's cavalry corps swept in to deliver a potentially decisive blow. At the same time, General Latour-Maubourg's IV Cavalry Corps destroyed a Russian grenadier division before it could deploy in square, only to be driven off by counterattacking Russian cavalry behind them. Further south, General Nansouty's I Cavalry Corps could make no headway against infantry of the Russian Imperial Guard, which had formed squares, while in Semenovskaya itself Russian grenadiers fought with such tenacity that only Murat's presence stopped the French from abandoning the place altogether.

Another French advance ejected the Russians from the burning village once again, and for a short time Kutusov's army was actually split in two. A second appeal to Napoleon to throw in the Imperial Guard was made and declined, and with it probably went the last opportunity for a breakthrough. Nor were Murat's cavalry properly put to use: the bulk of them, having been repulsed from the area around Semenovskaya, sat immobile for hours, receiving no orders to exploit the gap in the Russian line and suffering horrendous losses, including General Montbrun, commander of II Cavalry Corps, who was killed by Russian artillery fire. The Russians filled the gap, and, despite the loss of Semenovskaya and the *flêches*, Kutusov's line remained intact, albeit severely battered.

Meanwhile, Eugène, concentrating every available horseman, attempted to advance further after the fall of the Rayevsky Redoubt in order to exploit his success there, but Barclay de Tolly halted his advance by bringing up two fresh cavalry corps. With no further reserves, the French were simply unable to proceed further.

On the Russian right, Kutusov now showed some rare initiative, ordering a broad cavalry sweep intended to strike the French rear. Generals Uvarov and Platov, with regular cavalry and Cossacks totalling 8,000 horsemen, advanced with caution, and though they declined to attack the French rear, did manage to cause panic in their ranks and paralyze thousands of troops who might have been committed to the fray in the centre.

The Rayevsky Redoubt, the focus of hours of artillery fire by over 150 guns, remained to be vanquished. At about 1500hrs, the French launched a coordinated infantry and cavalry attack against the now-shapeless feature. Napoleon's aide-de-camp, General Caulaincourt, leading II and IV Cavalry Corps, advanced over the breastworks with the Saxon and Polish heavy cavalry, while French cuirassiers stormed in through the back. Caulaincourt was killed in the charge, but the key to Kutusov's line was taken, secured by infantry which stormed through the embrasures in the wake of the cavalry. There followed a two-hour cavalry engagement as French and allied regiments

In the wake of several failed attempts by infantry to take and hold the position, Saxon, Polish and French heavy cavalry charge over the ramparts of the Great Redoubt, by now pounded relentlessly by concentrated artillery fire. (Author's collection)

galloped on into the main Russian line, where Barclay de Tolly twice narrowly escaped death.

On Napoleon's extreme right, Poniatowski's Polish troops carried on the struggle and at 1600hrs were able to recapture Utitsa and the knoll on which it stood. However, the appearance of Russian reinforcements – unbeknownst to Poniatowski they were the Moscow militia, a force of very dubious quality – gave the attackers cause for concern, and the offensive ground to a halt. Indeed, by 1700hrs all along the front the fighting gradually petered out, both sides exhausted from the bloodletting. Large gaps had opened in the Russian line, but Napoleon continued to refuse to send in the Imperial Guard in what might have been a decisive turn of affairs. As the fighting abated, the French stood roughly on the site of the original Russian positions. Still, Kutusov's army, shaken though not broken, retired only a short distance away to the next ridge – hardly the outcome that Napoleon had desired.

Both sides were exhausted. Casualties were horrendous. Exact figures are not known, but approximately 44,000 Russians fell at Borodino, of whom perhaps 25,000 were wounded and left on the field. Bagration lay mortally wounded, Tuchkov was dead, and 21 other Russian generals were casualties. Some corps were so depleted as to be mistaken for divisions, and divisions for regiments. The French, for their part, held the field, but at a cost of about 33,000 wounded and killed – roughly 40 per cent of their original force. Montbrun and Caulaincourt were among the dead, and Davout was wounded. All told, about a dozen divisional generals and nearly 200 staff and senior officers were among the fallen. Too weary to pursue, the French withdrew to their original lines and had to content themselves with possession of a battlefield choked with bodies.

Napoleon had shown little imagination, with massacre the inevitable result of two armies slugging it out on a congested field. Both sides claimed victory, but Borodino may best be described as a draw or, arguably, a technical victory for the French, who, with the road open ahead of them, staggered into Moscow on 14 September. That said, Napoleon sustained losses on such a scale as to render Borodino a Pyrrhic victory. While Kutusov had certainly lost a considerable proportion of his forces, he could expect reinforcements, whereas the French could not rebuild the units that had been thrust in to the cauldron of fire with such lavish disregard for the losses they were bound to suffer. Nor could they easily replenish their expended ammunition. Thus, despite their Herculean efforts on 7 September, the French failed to achieve the decisive outcome they desired, marking Borodino as the climax of the campaign and the beginning of the end of the Grande Armée in Russia.

From Borodino to Waterloo, 1812–15

Although Napoleon achieved his aim of taking Moscow, no peace with Russia was agreed and the Grande Armée was forced to retreat from 19 October onwards. Fewer than 10,000 survivors eventually reached the river Niemen, marking the Polish frontier, at the end of December, when the Russians halted their pursuit of an army that had dissolved into mere rabble.

Notwithstanding the immense losses Napoleon suffered in Russia, his extraordinary administrative skills enabled him to rebuild his army by the spring of 1813. The Sixth Coalition, which had been formed by Britain, Russia and other powers in June 1812, now expanded to include Prussia. The Austrians as yet remained neutral when the spring campaign of 1813 opened. Napoleon occupied the Saxon capital, Dresden, on 7–9 May, and defeated General Wittgenstein, commanding the Russo-Prussian force, first at Lützen on 2 May and again at Bautzen on 20–21 May. Both sides agreed to an armistice, which stretched from June until mid-August, during which time Napoleon redoubled his recruitment drive and trained his green army, while the Allies assembled larger and larger forces, now at last including the Austrians and Swedes.

When the campaign resumed, the Allies deployed three multinational armies that defeated Napoleon's subordinates in three actions in August. Napoleon, for his part, scored a significant victory at Dresden on 26–27 August against Prince Schwarzenberg, the Allied commander-in-chief, but the Emperor failed to pursue the Austrian commander. Bavaria, the principal member of the Confederation of the Rhine, defected to the Allies, and the decisive battle of the campaign was fought at Leipzig from 16 to 19 October, when all three main Allied armies converged on the city to attack Napoleon's positions in and around it. In the largest battle in modern history hitherto, both sides suffered extremely heavy losses, though the Allies nevertheless achieved a victory of immense proportions that forced the French out of Germany and back across the Rhine.

Convinced that he could still recover his vast territorial losses, Napoleon chose to fight on against all odds, rejecting offers from the Allies that would have left France with its

Napoleon leading the remnants of his shattered troops during the retreat from Moscow. He left the army on 8 December to return to Paris in order to begin the painful process of rebuilding his forces for the inevitable confrontation against Russia and what allies she could muster in the spring of 1813. (Author's collection)

'natural' frontiers: the Rhine, the Alps and the Pyrenees. French forces were under pressure from all sides. Wellington's Anglo-Portuguese forces had already crossed the Pyrenees; the Austrians were already operating in northern Italy; and several armies were making seemingly inexorable progress into eastern France via Switzerland and Germany, and from the north through Holland. To oppose these impressive forces, Napoleon possessed little more than a small army consisting of hastily raised units, National Guardsmen and anyone who had somehow avoided the call-ups of the past. In spectacular fashion, at least in the initial stages of the campaign, the Emperor managed to summon up the kind of energy and tactical brilliance for which he had become renowned during the Italian campaigns of 1796–97.

Above: The retreat from Moscow. The debacle cost Napoleon not only an army, but ultimately his empire, as well. (Author's collection)

In swift succession he drubbed Blücher at Brienne on 29 January, at La Rothière on 30 January, at Champaubert on 10 February, at Montmirail on 11 February, at Château-Thierry on 12 February and at Vauchamps on 14 February. The Emperor then turned to confront Schwarzenberg at Montereau on 18 February, before again fighting Blücher, at Craonne, near Paris, on 7 March. Yet, however many enemies he could repel in turn, Napoleon could not be everywhere at once, and his corps commanders, despite the continued enthusiasm for battle displayed by the troops themselves, could not achieve the same results in the field as the Emperor.

While Napoleon was still 193km (120 miles) from the capital at St Dizier, the Allies encountered only token resistance around Montmartre on 30 March, where Marmont refused to fight on, allowing the Allies to enter the capital the following day. At a conference with his marshals, Napoleon found himself surrounded by men finally prepared to defy him; the troops, they declared, would listen to their generals, not the Emperor. With no alternative, Napoleon

Below: Napoleon arriving at the river Elbe, April 1813. The resumption of campaigning at the head of a newly created army in the wake of the Russian fiasco proved a testament to the Emperor's phenomenal capacity to raise and equip his forces. (Author's collection)

abdicated unconditionally on 11 April and took up residence on the tiny island of Elba, off the Italian coast, while the Bourbon line in France was restored under Louis XVIII.

Yet Napoleon was not content to remain on Elba. Landing in France in March 1815 with a small band of followers, he marched on Paris, gathering loyal veterans and adherents from the army as he went. Allied leaders were at the time assembled at Vienna, there to redraw the map of Europe that had been so radically revised by more than two decades of war. The Seventh Coalition was soon on the

Above: Napoleon resting in a French home during the Allied invasion of 1814. If the Emperor's campaigning between 1809 and 1813 marked a distinct shift from his 'glory years' of 1805–07, the crisis created by enemies crossing the Rhine spurred him to rekindle the energy and tactical brilliance of those earlier, halcyon days. (Author's collection)

march, with effectively the whole of Europe in arms and marching to defeat Napoleon before he could raise sufficient troops to hold off the overwhelming Allied numbers. With the speed characteristic of his earlier days in uniform, Napoleon quickly moved north to confront the only Allied forces within reach: an Anglo-Dutch army under Wellington and a Prussian one under Blücher, both in Belgium. Napoleon could only hope to survive against the massive onslaught that would soon reach France by defeating the Allied armies separately; to this end he sought to keep Wellington and Blücher – who together heavily outnumbered him – apart.

On 16 June, after a rapid march that caught Wellington entirely off guard, Napoleon detached Ney to seize the crossroads at Quatre Bras, then occupied by part of Wellington's army, while with the main body of the French army he moved to strike Blücher at Ligny. Ney failed in his objective, and though on the same day Napoleon delivered a sharp, though not crippling blow against the Prussians, the critical result was that the two Allied armies continued to remain within supporting distance of one another. In the aftermath of Ligny, Blücher, having promised to support Wellington if he were attacked by Napoleon's main body, took up a position at Wavre, while the duke deployed his tired but still intact army on a ridge just south of Mont St Jean, 18km (11 miles) to the west of the Prussian position.

Right: The Emperor bids farewell to the Imperial Guard at the Palace of Fontainebleau, April 1814, before departing for exile on Elba. (Author's collection)

Waterloo, 18 June 1815

Having detached Marshal Grouchy with 33,000 men to keep the Prussians occupied at Wavre, Napoleon established his army, now 72,000-strong, on a ridge just south of the Anglo-Allied position. Wellington had 68,000 men, comprising mainly mixed Anglo-Hanoverian and some Dutch-Belgian divisions. Most of these he placed along a 3km (2-mile) crescent-shaped ridge, though 18,000 were detached 8km (5 miles) west at Tubize, to prevent the French from making a wide sweep around to the west and so threatening his right flank. On Wellington's left stood the villages of Papelotte and La Haye. In his centre stood the farm of La Haye Sainte near the crossroads formed by the Ohain and Charleroi–Brussels roads. On his right, and somewhat forward of his main line, lay the château of Hougoumont, which included woods, farm buildings and a garden. Wellington recognized the tactical importance of Hougoumont and La Haye Sainte, and placed reliable garrisons in each. These strongpoints presented obstacles to a French attack on the Allied right and centre, and could offer enfilading fire to any opposing troops that sought to bypass them. Hougoumont was large enough, moreover, to make a sweep around Wellington's right more difficult, though not impossible.

In his effort to keep the Prussians and Anglo-Allies separated, on the morning of 17 June Napoleon had detached Grouchy to pursue the Prussians

Waterloo, situation about 1100hrs

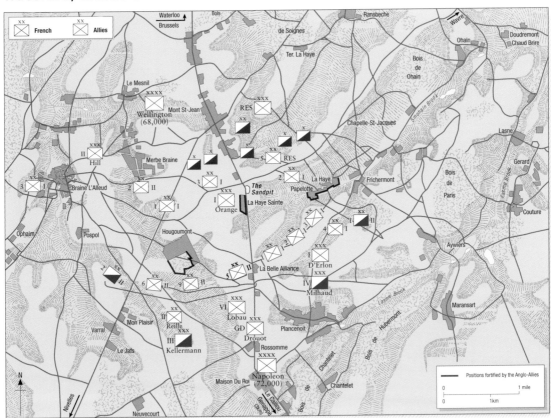

Marshal Emmanuel Grouchy, the scapegoat for Napoleon's defeat at Waterloo. The attribution is unfair, for he received no specific orders to reinforce the Emperor, whose ambiguous commands directed him to remain at Wavre. On this basis he refused to march to the sound of the guns. (Author's collection)

who, after their defeat at Ligny, had moved east towards Wavre. The Emperor was not aware that, though Grouchy would indeed engage part of the Prussian army on the 18th, Blücher, along with several corps, was then on the march to bolster Wellington's defence at Waterloo. Had Napoleon known this, perhaps he would not have opened the battle so late – around 1130hrs – as his plan to keep the Allied armies apart and defeat them in turn would have dictated that he defeat Wellington as early on the 18th as possible, before the Prussians could arrive to reinforce him. In the event, Napoleon waited for the rain-sodden ground to harden before opening his frontal attack, in spite of the presence of the heavily fortified farms at La Haye Sainte, Hougoumont and elsewhere. Wellington's dispositions might have suggested a different course to a more cautious attacker: either to withdraw and fight Wellington another day on a field of Napoleon's choosing, or to execute a wide outflanking manoeuvre so as to rob the duke of the advantages of his strong defensive position on the ridge. Instead, Napoleon sought to pierce the Anglo-Allied centre and take control of the slopes of Mont St-Jean, thus dividing Wellington's force in two and wresting control of the vital Brussels road – Wellington's main line of retreat and communication.

Napoleon opened the battle at 1130hrs with an attack by General Reille's corps on Hougoumont, whose capture was vital if the Emperor were to achieve victory, for so long as the Anglo-Allies held it, the French could not confidently threaten Wellington's right or centre-right. Situated 457m (500 yards) in front of the Allied line, along the crest of the ridge, Hougoumont remained a formidable obstacle to any major French advance. Reille's attack was intended as a diversion to force Wellington to weaken his line in order to reinforce the beleaguered farm complex.

Ironically, the French attack throughout the day drew in more and more French troops in a fruitless effort to take the stronghold. In the course of the battle, fewer than 3,000 British, Hanoverians and Nassauers fended off almost 13,000 French troops, making Hougoumont a virtually separate engagement within the greater context of the battle. The French briefly managed to force open the gate of the farmyard, but a handful of men from the Coldstream Guards shut it before the assailants could break in and overwhelm the defenders. In the course of the day, the French lost large numbers of troops outside the walls and in the woods adjacent during the eight hours of fighting that took place there.

By 1330hrs Prussian troops under General Bülow began to arrive, at first in small numbers, on Wellington's left flank. Napoleon, unaware of precisely how many Prussians Grouchy had held up at Wavre, decided that no more time could be lost, and ordered the Comte d'Erlon to advance with his corps of 16,000 men against the Allied centre-left. The troops marched 1,189m (1,300 yards) under artillery fire and captured the hamlet of Papelotte, while a detached brigade attacked La Haye Sainte, seizing the garden and orchard from its Hanoverian defenders. The French made no attempt to set fire to the roof with their howitzers or bring up enough artillery to make a breach in the wall; the defenders therefore clung on, though heavily outnumbered. D'Erlon's men had reached as far as the crest of the ridge, driving off a Dutch-Belgian brigade in the process, when General Sir Thomas Picton, commanding the 5th Division, ordered a bayonet attack in the wake of a destructive fusillade. Picton was killed, but his infantry was supported by a strong body of cavalry, including the Union and Household brigades, sent forward by Lord Uxbridge, commander of the Anglo-Allied cavalry.

Marshal Michel Ney. One of Napoleon's greatest commanders, Ney's squandering of the heavy cavalry reserve at Waterloo nevertheless comprised one of a number of avoidable blunders committed in the battle. (Author's collection)

The attacking horsemen pushed aside opposing cavalry protecting d'Erlon's left flank and, surprising the infantry, fell upon it with great ferocity, driving them back down the slope in total confusion and taking 2,000 prisoners. Yet, as had happened on several occasions in Spain, the British failed to maintain proper discipline, and rather than stop, re-form and return to friendly lines, they galloped on in unrestrained excitement, sabring many of the gunners of the massed battery the French had established at the beginning of the battle, but penetrating perilously deep into enemy lines. General Ponsonby found himself unable to control his men, and the French pounced on them with lancers and cuirassiers from both flanks, leaving more than a third of the British cavalry wounded or killed, including Ponsonby himself. Only 1,000 troopers returned out of a force of 2,500. While much of the British cavalry had been put out of action for the remainder of the day, d'Erlon's force, which represented a quarter of the French at Waterloo, had been disastrously repulsed, with 25 per cent losses and 2,000 men captured. Had he succeeded, d'Erlon might have won the day then and there. Napoleon now had to find another method.

Meanwhile, the defenders of Hougoumont continued to fend off the ferocious attacks of Jérôme Napoleon's infantry, while at the same time the Hanoverians clung on at La Haye Sainte. The Prussians began to arrive in gradually increasing numbers from Wavre, and Picton's division withdrew back to friendly lines, not making the same mistake as the cavalry. By 1500hrs, apart from the fighting around Hougoumont and La Haye Sainte, the battle entered a lull, as both sides needed a respite in which to consider their next moves. About this time Grouchy began to hear the sound of the guns at Waterloo. Strictly adhering to his instructions to pursue the Prussians to Wavre and to keep them pinned there, and ignoring the entreaties of his staff officers to march immediately to the sound of the guns – where it was correctly presumed the Emperor was engaging Wellington – Grouchy continued to engage the Prussian rearguard of 15,000 men left at Wavre and ignored the departure of their other formations. This was to prove a fatal error for the French, for by 1630hrs the bulk of Blücher's forces were arriving on Wellington's left in large numbers.

The French now attempted another grand stroke – this time with their cavalry – at about 1530hrs, once d'Erlon's corps had regrouped and assembled itself back in the line. A renewed attempt at seizing La Haye Sainte, this time under the personal direction of Ney, failed. With the grand battery's losses from Uxbridge's attack now replaced, the French resumed their bombardment of the Allied lines, where many regiments were ordered to lie down for protection. Even still, artillery fire took a heavy toll on Wellington's men on the ridge. Ney now sought to clear that position by launching a massive cavalry attack, unsupported by infantry, totalling about 5,000 men.

The attack fell on the infantry deployed between Hougoumont and La Haye Sainte. But the defenders had formed square – the classic formation for defence against mounted attack – with several ranks of infantry deployed back-to-back in the form of a square, bristling with bayonets presented in the direction of the enemy on all sides, and thus virtually immune from direct assault by men on horseback. Whereas a square was extremely vulnerable to combined-arms attack, particularly artillery at close range, the French cavalry appeared on the ridge practically unaccompanied, there to confront a wall of impenetrable bayonets behind which stood men beyond the reach of sword and sabre, firing their muskets with virtual impunity. More and more cavalry – in the end amounting to some 80 squadrons or 10,000 men – were committed to these futile attacks. The onslaught proved so ineffective that many British soldiers were relieved to hear the sound of the trumpets announcing each fresh attack, since approaching cavalry forced the French to cease the fire of their artillery lest they should strike their own advancing horsemen. Still, some Anglo-Allied squares suffered heavy casualties at the hands of the few batteries of horse artillery that did manage to accompany the cavalry.

Yet it was the attackers who suffered the most, for wave after wave could do little more than swirl ineffectively around the squares before receding back down the slope, their horses blown and many men and their mounts lost to musket and artillery fire. Indeed, British gunners often discharged their cannon at short range before taking refuge inside the squares. Once the attackers withdrew, the gunners would re-man their guns and prepare for the next onslaught. Ney's cavalry charges – perhaps a dozen or more – continued for about two hours, between 1530 and 1730hrs, but all in vain, for not only did the horsemen fail to penetrate the squares, the bodies of their fallen comrades and mounts choked the field and impeded the progress of the regiments behind. Wellington's squares all held fast, and the French grew weary, with many regiments executing the last charges at hardly more than a trot.

While Ney's cavalry fruitlessly assaulted the infantry squares, the Prussians under Bülow and Gneisenau were arriving on Napoleon's right flank,

Waterloo, situation about 1800hrs

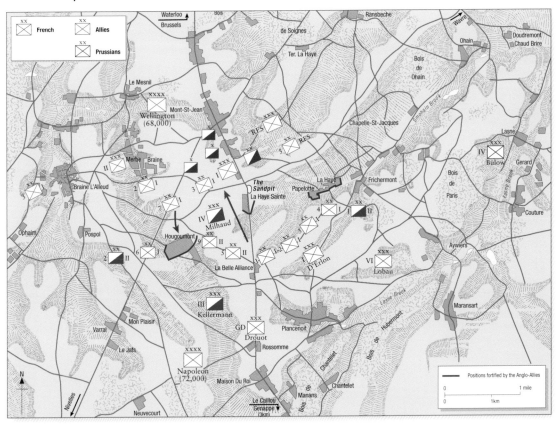

particularly around Frichermont, where Comte Lobau was sent to hold them back while the main French effort continued to concentrate on breaking Wellington's centre. Bülow's 30,000 men engaged Lobau's 10,000 defenders in furious fighting in and around the Bois de Paris and Frichermont, out of which Lobau was driven towards the village of Plancenoit. Overwhelmed by superior numbers, Lobau was eventually ejected from Plancenoit, as well, obliging Napoleon to send in the Young Guard to retake the place, which they did shortly before 1900hrs.

By this time the corps of generals Pirch and Zieten had also arrived from the east, on Wellington's flank, boosting the morale of the battered Anglo-Allies, disheartening the French who were aware of the Prussians' arrival, and drawing away more of Napoleon's reserves that might have been used against Wellington's centre. With the tide turning in the duke's favour and the Prussians arriving to bolster his left, Wellington was able to withdraw some of his forces from his extreme left and shift them to his vulnerable centre. This was all the more necessary as infantry from the French reserve were beginning to mass around La Belle Alliance, readying themselves for another great attack on the Anglo-Allied centre and centre-right; specifically, against the tiny garrison still holding out in La Haye Sainte.

Napoleon at Waterloo. With the armies arrayed on the field virtually identical in number, it was imperative to French success that the Emperor made the best use of his forces, whether or not Blücher could aid Wellington with reinforcements. At this he catastrophically failed. (Author's collection)

Major Baring and his Hanoverian infantry had been reinforced periodically with Nassauers, but in the course of six hours' fighting, his riflemen had received no new stocks of ammunition, and by 1800hrs were desperately short and unable to continue to resist their assailants with anything more than sword bayonets and musket butts. The French, moreover, had set the roof of the farmhouse on fire, and some time between 1800 and 1830hrs the remaining 42 infantry out of the original 400 defenders were obliged to abandon the post. This was an important tactical success for Napoleon, for La Haye Sainte stood firmly in the Anglo-Allied centre, offering possession of the strategically important Charleroi–Brussels road. The moment was a critical one for Wellington, for if Napoleon could exploit this opportunity before the full force of the Prussians could be felt, the Emperor still stood a chance of seizing the day. Ney therefore brought up artillery and pounded the line at close range, repulsed an attempt to retake the farmhouse, and forced out riflemen deployed in the sandpit near La Haye Sainte.

The moment had arrived for the French to appear in force: yet they could not do so. Thousands were still engaged around Hougoumont and could not be withdrawn quickly enough, even if the order had been issued. D'Erlon's formation, though certainly not eliminated from the fighting, was exhausted and in no state to switch to the offensive. Meanwhile, to the south-east, Bülow's corps had by now retaken Plancenoit, ejecting the Young Guard in bitter house-to-house fighting that exposed the French right flank and brought the Prussians to within 2km of La Belle Alliance in the French centre. There were no available reserves for Ney, despite his pleas, apart from the Middle Guard and Old Guard, which Napoleon refused to commit.

Wellington for his part remained in a perilous state, riding up and down the line reassuring his men and ordering no withdrawals for any reason lest it cause a panic and general retreat. While gaps – some of them quite large – appeared along Wellington's line, Napoleon declined to gamble on striking a potentially deadly blow, notwithstanding the pounding his artillery had inflicted on the Anglo-Allied forces.

The Prussians, meanwhile, carried on pushing forward into Napoleon's right flank, bringing their artillery close enough even to hit the Charleroi road down which any French retreat was likely to pass. Napoleon sensed the crisis and ordered two battalions of the Old Guard to capture Plancenoit with the bayonet. Within half an hour this elite infantry had evicted many times their number of Prussians, enabling the Young Guard to re-establish their former positions in the devastated village, by then choked with dead and wounded. When the Old Guard carried on beyond Plancenoit, however, Bülow's superior numbers began to tell, and the French were driven back. Nevertheless, the Emperor's favourites had given him a respite, and this, with the fall of La Haye Sainte and the wavering Anglo-Allied centre, left one last opportunity for Napoleon to defeat Wellington.

Time was short for the Emperor, for much as the Imperial Guard could halt, if temporarily, the Prussian advance against his right, they were powerless to stop the tide of Prussians linking up with the Anglo-Allies on Wellington's left. If he was to deliver a decisive blow against his opponent Napoleon had to strike soon. He still had at his disposal 5,000 fresh infantry of the Middle and Old Guard. Brought forward at the right point along the Allied line, these veterans might yet turn the tide of victory in Napoleon's favour. First, in order to bolster his men's morale, the Emperor circulated false reports that the troops arriving on the French right were in fact Grouchy's and not Blücher's. Then, at around 1900hrs he sent forward the Guard infantry – five battalions in the first wave and three in the second, under Ney. The first wave received support from troops of d'Erlon's corps, plus cavalry and artillery of the Guard. Aware of the impending attack and with 15 minutes in which to prepare to receive it, Wellington closed up his line and deployed cavalry to the rear to prevent any possible breakthrough.

As the sun was setting at about 1930hrs, the Guard marched in columns up the ridge and attacked a point about equidistant between Hougoumont and La Haye Sainte. At the top of the ridge 30 cannon stood to receive them; the case shot fired exacted a heavy toll on the attackers. Undeterred, the Guard continued its advance, driving off Brunswickers and British infantry, and capturing some artillery. Yet when a Dutch-Belgian battery fired at close range, followed by a bayonet attack made by 3,000 Dutch-Belgian infantry, a battalion of the Guard was driven back down the slope. Another battalion of the Old Guard struck General Halkett's brigade, but its two fresh British regiments remained steadfast and then repulsed their assailants with musket fire and the support of a nearby horse artillery battery. The first French wave had thus failed.

The Imperial Guard surrounded in the closing phase of Waterloo. This depicts the famous scene of defiance by General Cambronne who, when summoned to surrender, is said to have declared, 'The Guard dies, but does not surrender!' In reality he is thought to have blurted out an expletive of a scatological nature. (Author's collection)

Now came the turn of three battalions of the Chasseurs of the Middle Guard. These had been subjected to intense artillery fire since they had begun their advance from La Belle Alliance and ascended the ridge toward the Ohain road. Suddenly, on Wellington's command, from out of the corn rose the 1st Foot Guards, hitherto lying prone. The ensuing devastating volley stopped the attackers in their tracks. At the same time they were subjected to case shot at under 183m (200 yards). After ten minutes of this intense fire, the French began to waver, whereupon Wellington ordered the Foot Guards to charge with the bayonet. On this, the Chasseurs retreated down the slopes past Hougoumont and back whence they had come. Finally, another battalion of the Middle Guard advanced up the ridge, to be met by various units, including two British brigades and the Hanoverians out of Hougoumont, all of whom fired on the attackers from various directions. But the final straw came when a light infantry battalion appeared on the Guards' left flank and fired a volley at pointblank range. The remainder of the brigade then charged with the bayonet, driving the Chasseurs away.

Wellington, seeing that the moment of victory had arrived, rode to the top of the ridge and waved his hat in the air to signal a general advance across the entire front. With the repulse of Napoleon's ultimate reserve, the fatal words '*La Garde recule!*' (the Guard recoils!) spread like wildfire down the French ranks, and the army rapidly began to dissolve into a fleeing mass. Some of the hitherto uncommitted units of the Guard stood firm in square, but after taking severe punishment from musket and artillery fire at close range, these too broke and ran, following their comrades in headlong flight. The fate of Napoleon's army was sealed by pursuing Prussian cavalry, who rode down thousands of men before darkness set in.

Waterloo led to Napoleon's final downfall, restored the balance of power in Europe and ushered in an era of nearly four decades of peace on the Continent, unquestionably qualifying the battle as one of history's most decisive.

Napoleon at Waterloo

By this time the Emperor was but a shadow of his former self: wearied by years of campaigning, a year in exile and – on the day of battle itself – ill. He had long since passed his peak, a fact highlighted by the series of blunders he himself made or allowed Ney to make, including his failure to keep the two Allied armies separated after Quatre Bras and Ligny on the 16th; waiting to commence action at Waterloo under the mistaken impression that the ground would sufficiently harden to enable his artillery to inflict maximum damage on Wellington's infantry; conceding the initiative by allowing the duke to establish himself on highly defensible ground of his own choosing; diverting too many troops to the attack on Hougoumont and failing to deploy his artillery against it; sacrificing his best cavalry in fruitless attacks against infantry deployed in square; and, finally, refusing immediately to commit his Imperial Guard reserve against the gap created in the Anglo-Allied centre by the fall of La Haye Sainte. Thus, by the time he ordered his men forward, as depicted here, Wellington had stabilized his line and the brief window of opportunity was no more.

OPPOSING COMMANDERS

In the course of his long military career Napoleon fought a host of rival commanders, with names too numerous to mention, but amongst the most prominent of whom three emerge as particularly worthy of note, having commanded armies of their own in the battles specifically detailed in the previous section: the Russian commander, General, later Field Marshal, Mikhail Kutusov; the Prussian commander, General, later Field Marshal, Gebhard Blücher, and Lieutenant-General, later Field Marshal, Sir Arthur Wellesley, better known, of course, as the Duke of Wellington.

Kutusov

As discussed earlier, Kutusov commanded one of the two Russian armies serving in the campaign of 1805, fighting in minor actions at Lambach, Amstetten and Dürnstein. After withdrawing to Olmütz, he advised a withdrawal east, there to await Russian reinforcements, only to find himself overruled by the Tsar and his staff, who despite the Austrian capitulation at Ulm in October and the fatigue of the Russian army as a result of its lengthy march to Moravia, wished to engage the French at the earliest opportunity. The result was as described in detail: together with the Austrians, the Russians under Kutusov suffered a catastrophic defeat at Austerlitz on 2 December, leading to the retreat of the Tsar's forces through Hungary and back into Russia. Kutusov did not participate in the campaign of 1807 in Poland and East Prussia, but re-emerged with a significant command in 1811 during the conflict with Turkey, against whom he led the (Russian) Army of Moldavia. He crushed the Turkish Army in July, so contributing to the favourable treaty of peace in May 1812 that enabled Russia to withdraw substantial forces from her southern theatre of operations to oppose the far greater threat of Napoleon's invasion.

At the start of the campaign Kutusov commanded the St Petersburg militia and later led its counterpart in Moscow, while command of the two principal Russian armies lay with Barclay de Tolly and Bagration. In the wake of the French capture of Smolensk, however, Alexander felt obliged to satisfy the public's demand for Kutusov's reinstatement to a prominent position and duly appointed him commander-in-chief of all the Russian armies. In this new role, Kutusov adopted a simple, straightforward strategy of attrition: to wear down Napoleon's vast army by fighting a series of minor but harassing engagements followed in turn by retreat, so enabling Russian forces to remain intact and ready to fight again. Kutusov's plan, however, faced mounting criticism from his subordinates and the Russian populace, who insisted that he make a stand before Moscow, which he duly did at Borodino on 7 September, resulting in horrendous casualties on both sides and the French sufficiently exhausted from the blood-letting as to be incapable of immediate pursuit. Kutusov decided to abandon Moscow, but with reinforcements continuing to swell his ranks and by shifting his forces so as to prevent Napoleon from obtaining desperately needed supplies from southern Russia,

Kutusov contributed much to Napoleon's fateful decision to retreat in the midst of winter after the Russian commander rejected his proposal to negotiate.

During Napoleon's retreat from Moscow, Kutusov blocked the Emperor's path at Maloyaroslavets and after a brief fight succeeded in diverting his opponent's route along the same line of march which the French had taken during their advance the previous summer, so condemning Napoleon to withdraw over territory long-since stripped bare of supplies and accommodation. Kutusov then shifted to the offensive, striking the French at Viazma, Liakhovo and Krasnyi, though he did not pursue with vigour, being careful not to engage in a major pitched engagement, preferring to allow the increasingly severe weather and the dearth of food to wear down his opponents. This reluctance enabled much of the remnant of Napoleon's army to cross the icy waters of the Berezina River in late November – albeit at considerable cost – ultimately to reach safety across the Russian frontier. Nevertheless, the Tsar congratulated Kutusov on his success in the campaign and promoted him.

Mikhail Kutusov, the best-known Russian commander of the Napoleonic era who, like his contemporaries, possessed few of the qualities most associated with outstanding generalship. (Courtesy of Alexander Mikaberidze)

The new field marshal respectfully opposed the Tsar's plan to pursue the French into East Prussia and the Duchy of Warsaw, but when Alexander reached the army during its advance through Polish territory, his superior rank automatically elevated him to overall command. By this time, in any event, Kutusov had fallen gravely ill and he died on 28 April 1813, commemorated as a hero in Russia ever since.

The best known of a host of Russian commanders who fought Napoleon, Kutusov may be summed up as a sound strategist who appreciated that while during the campaign of 1812 he possessed a formidable army under him, it nevertheless could do little better than exchange approximately equal casualties with Napoleon, against whom it could be most effectively employed once the Emperor's faulty strategy led to disastrous retreat.

Blücher

The Prussian Army's most charismatic and popular field commander, General Gebhard Lebrecht von Blücher, embodied a strong will, iron discipline and colourful leadership, most prominently in the campaigns of 1813–15. A bluff, heavy drinker and smoker, he sported the air of an non-commissioned officer and the temper of a bulldog. He had no head for strategy – which he left to the intellectuals on his competent staff – but was imbued with a great sense of *élan* like a true cavalryman, was always keen to ride into battle at the head of his troops, oblivious to personal danger. Such traits stood him in good stead amongst his soldiers, who admired his aggression and bravery.

Although a veteran of the French Revolutionary Wars, Blücher's first contact with Napoleon's troops came during the 1806 campaign when, at the head of a cavalry formation at Auerstädt, he launched a series of futile attacks against numerically superior infantry. During the retreat of Prussian forces in the wake of the twin disasters of Jena and Auerstädt, Blücher, almost unique among corps commanders, did not fall into discord with his subordinates and managed – ably assisted by his chief of staff, General Gerhard von Scharnhorst – to withdraw in good order while attempting to hold off pursuing French forces. While most Prussian commanders chose to surrender even where tactical circumstances did not require it, in contrast, Blücher capitulated near Lübeck only after he secured from the opposing commander a formal recognition that with his supplies utterly exhausted there remained no alternative.

With his honour intact but Prussia thereafter groaning under French occupation, Blücher remained inactive and despondent while others engaged in sweeping domestic reforms of the country, including its army. Blücher saw his chance to resume service in the field when, in 1813, Prussia again took up the sword of resistance with its forces substantially better armed and trained as a result of the work of Scharnhorst, Gneisenau, Clausewitz and others. Scharnhorst, who played a prominent part in ensuring that Blücher returned to the field, again assumed his former position as the general's chief of staff, maintaining a high level of efficiency within the army. Blücher played an important part in the battle of Lützen in May 1813, personally leading his troops in the fray and sustaining a minor wound. He fought again at Bautzen later that month, and though in each case Napoleon could claim victory, neither action could qualify as decisive, and with Blücher's forces increasing in number and their commander steadfast in pursuit of the enemy, the Prussians demonstrated their commitment to prosecute operations to a successful conclusion almost entirely on the strength of Blücher's indomitable character alone.

After fighting renewed following the summer armistice, Blücher commanded the Army of Silesia, one of the three principal Allied formations. Scharnhorst had since died of an infection contracted from a wound received at Bautzen, to be replaced by Gneisenau, but Blücher remained an inspirational commander of the highest order. At the Katzbach River on 26 August, he exhibited his characteristically high degree of aggression, seriously defeating Marshal Macdonald and playing a prominent part in the colossal battle of Leipzig in October, where he maintained unremitting pressure against Napoleon's army. Blücher was nothing if not a man of action, who continuously urged on his men during the advance towards the Rhine, crossing it on 31 December. During the campaign of 1814 in France he fought more engagements than any other Allied commander – often confronting forces under Napoleon's personal command – and though he frequently failed on a tactical level, notably at Champaubert, Montmirail, Château-Thierry and Vauchamps, his outstanding leadership and inspirational skills ensured that his soldiers' morale remained high and the spirit of the offensive undiminished.

After Napoleon's exile to Elba, Blücher remained in command of the main Prussian army, at that time posted as a force of observation in Belgium, together with an Anglo-Allied army under Wellington, when the Emperor returned during the Hundred Days in 1815. Blücher was badly defeated two days before Waterloo at Ligny, where while personally leading a cavalry charge he had his horse shot from under him, leaving him pinned to the ground and nearly resulting in his capture by French cavalry, which rode over him without recognizing the potential prize. Yet, as discussed, Ligny did not constitute a decisive defeat, and in retreating to Wavre Blücher remained determined to fulfil his promise to march to his ally's aid in the event of another encounter.

Two days later, when Napoleon again confronted the duke, Blücher left only a rearguard to contain Grouchy and marched his forces through the rain toward the Anglo-Allied line, thus arriving with tens of thousands of troops to support Wellington's left flank and engage the French right at the village of Plancenoit, so obliging Napoleon to detach most of his reserve to stem the tide of the Prussian advance. The arrival of Blücher's men and the pressure they exerted on this unexpected sector of the French line, forced Napoleon to accelerate his efforts to defeat Wellington and ultimately frustrated his attempts to snatch victory before the Allies could unite their forces. The extent to which Blücher may be said to have turned the tide of battle remains a subject of considerable controversy, but at the very least he enabled Wellington to assume the offensive once Anglo-Allied infantry and artillery repulsed the attack of the Imperial Guard in the early evening.

Field Marshal Blücher. With no conception of higher strategy, the charismatic if crude Prussian commander placed more reliance on the cold steel of the bayonet and the spirit of the offensive than the niceties of creative manoeuvre to prosecute his campaigns. (Author's collection)

Wellington

Although Wellington only faced Napoleon once in battle, by confronting a host of his marshals and generals in Portugal, Spain and southern France he has justifiably become known as the one of the Emperor's greatest opponents. Thus, in assessing Wellington's leadership qualities, one must inevitably examine his record in the Peninsular War, with Waterloo marking the climax of a career whose foundations were laid in India before maturing in Iberia.

The high professional standards that the Anglo-Portuguese army achieved in Spain and Portugal were a testament to Wellington's abilities not only as a superb commander in the field, but also as a highly skilled administrator. His constant concern for the welfare of his men earned his troops' respect and, later devotion, though it could not be said that Wellington was loved like Napoleon. Indeed, the duke stood largely aloof socially, dressed in sober fashion, demanded strict discipline, never hesitated to order punishments – including death – for infractions, worked extremely long hours, and expected the same commitment to duty of his staff, which for the most part rendered him excellent service. Wellington also possessed remarkable stamina and made industrious use of his time. He would rise at 0600hrs and work until midnight, writing large numbers of orders and dispatches, and rode between 50 and 130km a day. In the six years he spent in the Peninsula he never once went on leave.

Wellington's supreme self-confidence about his plans and his abilities was tempered by an understanding of his limitations based on clear-sighted forward planning and good use of intelligence. He began the war with a well-conceived and effective long-term strategy in mind and he adapted his tactics to suit the ground, his opponents' strengths and weaknesses, and the capabilities of his men. He possessed the sort of mind that could quickly assess a situation, whether at the strategic or tactical level. He laid his plans carefully and often anticipated those of his enemy. He had a good grasp of logistics and understood that an effective army required regular supplies of food, equipment and ammunition. As such, he recognized the importance of an efficiently run commissariat.

Wellington seldom delegated authority to his subordinates and maintained personal control of affairs whenever possible, particularly on the battlefield. His orders were clear and he saw to it that they were carried out precisely. While his failure to delegate may be seen as a fault, his consistent battlefield successes – over a dozen, in fact – owed much to his presence on the scene, where by exposing himself to fire he encouraged his men and could see at first hand where action needed to be taken: sending reinforcements, exploiting a success, withdrawing and so on. Proof of his constant presence in the thick of things is shown by his narrow escape from capture on three occasions and the three times when he was hit by musket balls – though without receiving serious injury.

Wellington recognized, and acknowledged early in the war, that with only one army – and a small one at that – he could not afford to be defeated: he simply could not enjoy that luxury. Criticisms levelled against him as a strategically 'defensive' general should be analyzed in this light. He spent the years 1808–11 in a largely defensive posture and seldom took risks, fighting only when circumstances were favourable and then with positive results. By preventing the French from concentrating their massive numbers against him, he could fight their armies separately on reasonable terms and wait for the time to switch to the offensive.

Thus, though the French had several hundred thousand men in the Peninsula at any given time, Wellington normally fought battles with about 50,000 men on each side. Napoleon's invasion of Russia, in particular, enabled him to do so, since that campaign not only required some French troops to transfer east, but would later deny to French commanders in the Peninsula much-needed reinforcements. From then on the French were obliged to fight a two-front war, thereby emboldening Wellington to move to the offensive.

Wellington understood that the war in the Peninsula would be long, and where other commanders might have regarded the odds as hopeless, he persisted. If his campaigns failed, he would accept responsibility, and he understood his dependence on the goodwill and cooperation of his hosts. He never gave in to what he called 'the croakers', officers in his own army who suggested, often behind the scenes, that the war was a lost cause.

He inherited an army that, though it had undergone reforms under competent men like Sir Ralph Abercromby and Sir John Moore, had a poor military record. Yet in the course of a few years he organized and trained the finest fighting force of its size in Europe. And, whatever one may say about the contribution made by the Spanish – both regulars and guerrillas – the balance of Allied victory or defeat in the Peninsula ultimately hung on the ability of Wellington's army to defeat the French in the field. This he achieved consistently with small numbers that usually varied between 30,000 and 60,000 men of mixed nationality – but men of exceptionally high calibre, training and leadership.

In short, Wellington's consistent victories owed much to his careful planning, his personal supervision of the fighting, and his ability to react appropriately as circumstances changed. He anticipated the actions of his adversaries, who were often experienced generals, and so could plan accordingly. Finally, he commanded an army composed, in the main, of competent general officers and well-trained men, the best Britain has ever produced, with the possible exception of the British Expeditionary Force in 1914. His successes were not entirely unbroken: the siege of Burgos in 1812 stands out as the exception, while Badajoz, though successfully taken, proved an extremely costly affair, but few commanders of any age enjoyed the succession of victories for which Wellington may rightfully claim credit, and in this respect he stands close in estimation to the great Napoleon himself.

Field Marshal the Duke of Wellington, Napoleon's greatest nemesis. Although the two men did not meet until the fateful day of Waterloo, Wellington's campaigns of 1808–14 in Iberia and southern France played an important part in diverting more than 200,000 of Napoleon's forces from other fronts. (Author's collection)

INSIDE THE MIND

Napoleon was a man of great complexity, about whose character millions of words have been devoted in order to plunge the depths of an individual who assumed such multifarious roles in the course of his career: military commander above all, but also head of state, social reformer, law-giver, patron of the arts and private individual. Space permits here but an inkling into his character, whose salient features cannot be said to be attractive, for amidst a mind which contemporaries recognized as extraordinary for the retention of the tiniest of details – the name of a simple soldier met on a battlefield a decade earlier, the position of a minor unit on the periphery of an engagement, the amount of grain supplied to a brigade, the strength and composition of a formation in a distant theatre of operations – may also be said to dwell deep-seated notions of self-delusion and self-promotion bordering on egomania.

From his early years in uniform Napoleon believed he was destined for greatness and, once in power, crafted the machinery of state propaganda to encourage personal devotion and admiration for all aspects of his achievements – military, political, social and economic. He loved to issue grandiloquent statements before and after battle, taking considerable licence with the truth and invariably championing himself as the archetypal inspirational and charismatic leader, as his bulletins, correspondence and speeches attest. He went to great lengths to inculcate amongst his subjects a sense of allegiance not merely to the state but to himself personally, creating a cult status as exemplified in the Imperial Catechism, whereby the French people, genuine adherents or not, found themselves effectively obliged to swear an oath to him personally. Napoleon was an unashamed self-publicist whose power rested on his extraordinary capacity to captivate his soldiers with his undoubted charisma and to win the hearts of the French people at large by feeding them on that heady diet whose appeal the revolutionary generation could scarcely resist: *la Gloire* – glory achieved on the battlefield.

But glory is sometimes elusive and always fleeting, and when his campaigns failed, such as in Spain, the Emperor blamed his subordinates, whom he consistently accused of mismanagement and refusing to obey his directives sent from afar, only highlighting the fact that he did not understand conditions on the ground. Even where he was present on campaign, such as in Russia, Napoleon refused to accept responsibility for the disaster that befell him, to his deputies in Paris tersely explaining away the lives of half a million men in a single sentence: 'My army has sustained losses, but that is due to the harshness of the season.' If in the more intimate surroundings of his ministerial chamber he deigned to admit failure, he nevertheless dismissed the catastrophe with almost equal brevity to those assembled: 'I have made a great error, but I have the means of repairing it.' Thus, no sooner did Napoleon offer a sober appreciation of reality than he swiftly and with considerable powers of delusion declared his unshakeable faith that all would be well in due course. That his wars cost France the flower of a generation scarcely gave him pause for thought, as his harangue to Prince Metternich, the Austrian foreign minister, in the summer of 1813 testifies: 'I grew up on a battlefield and when one has done that one cares little for the lives of a million men.'

Publicly, of course, he made no such declarations. Indeed, he assiduously masked his losses by shamelessly manipulating casualty figures from the front – exaggerating

Napoleon in 1815. A man of remarkable political instincts and unquestioned military genius, had he appreciated the limits of his abilities France might have continued to hold sway over much of Europe for a substantial period, extending liberal reforms beyond even the Low Countries, Switzerland, Germany and Italy. (Author's collection)

enemy losses and minimizing those of his own. Thus, after his first defeat, at Aspern-Essling in 1809, he claimed casualties of 4,100 men when the true figure stood at nearly ten times that number. It is perhaps unsurprising that such travesties of the truth, published in *Le Moniteur*, the official government organ in Paris, earned for the Emperor such a woeful reputation for inaccuracy that the expression, 'To lie like a bulletin' became proverbial across France.

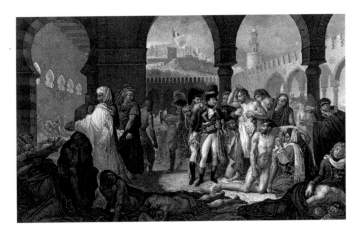

Above: Napoleon visiting victims of plague in hospital at Jaffa during the campaign in Syria, 1799. Notwithstanding occasions like this, compassion for the sufferings of his troops does not figure as a Napoleonic hallmark. (Author's collection)

In analyzing Napoleon's conduct and reading his voluminous correspondence one could be excused for detecting strong evidence of self-delusion. He refused to appreciate the magnitude of the Russian disaster even as it unfolded around him; he failed to accept that Wellington was capable of ousting French forces from Spain and continued to regard the conflict as an affair of guerrillas and not a major conventional front in its own right; and when in 1813 circumstances had clearly shifted radically against him and defeat became inevitable, the Emperor could still have settled on a reasonable peace, as offered by the Allies, and yet refused it repeatedly. Thus, in June of that year, during the armistice, he ostentatiously rejected an Allied peace plan by which France would have retained control over the Confederation of the Rhine, northern Italy, the Low Countries and Switzerland – the great bulk of the Empire. Not only did the threat of Austria joining the Allies not sway him, he viewed with contempt the notion that the combined weight of the three great Continental powers could dislodge him from central Europe, even in light of his disastrous campaign in Russia the previous year and the indecisive nature of the fighting in the spring of 1813.

Again, in November, Napoleon rejected a revised though not unreasonable peace proposal, on the basis of a French withdrawal within her 'natural

Below: Napoleon at the tomb of Frederick the Great, whose martial genius the Emperor greatly admired. (Author's collection)

frontiers' – the Alps, the Pyrenees and the Rhine – more than generous terms considering his predicament. Even after the Allies had crossed the Rhine in January 1814 they offered France her 'natural frontiers' once again, but when Napoleon achieved a series of minor victories in the first week of February he became blinkered to reality and foolishly emboldened, insisting to his ministers that such territorial strictures spelled disgrace for France. The delusion only continued: by mid-March, with the fall of the

Napoleon at the battle of Lützen, which marked the opening engagement of the 1813 campaign in Germany against Russia and Prussia. Note how, in the foreground, wounded friend and foe alike hail the Emperor, such being the respect in which he was held. (Author's collection)

capital looming, he wrote to the Allies demanding the evacuation of France and offering to withdraw from all territories beyond its borders.

It took the towering personality of Ney, whose record of service spoke for itself, to make the point in blunt terms: 'The army will not march,' he stated grimly. 'The army will obey me,' Napoleon insisted. 'The army will obey its generals,' Ney responded with defiance, delivering the *coup de grâce* and the signal that the authority of the Emperor was no more.

WHEN WAR IS DONE

On surrendering to the British in the wake of his second abdication after Waterloo, Napoleon went aboard HMS *Bellerophon*, appealing to the Prince Regent for quiet, undisturbed residence in the English countryside. But the British Government had no intention of permitting the possibility of the erstwhile Emperor's return to France as had occurred after Elba, and chose to exile him on the remote, volcanic South Atlantic island of St Helena, about 1,900km (1,200 miles) from the west coast of Africa. HMS *Northumberland* arrived at the island, defended by a garrison of 3,000 troops, on 16 October 1815, putting Napoleon ashore together with several members of the Imperial household, including Emmanuel, comte de Las Cases and Henri Bertrand, to be lodged at a private estate called Longwood, several kilometres from the capital, Jamestown.

Opposite: Napoleon's remains arriving in Paris from St Helena, 1840. The growth of the Napoleonic myth by this time would help propel his nephew, Louis-Napoleon, into power in 1848 as president of the Second Republic and, in 1852, as the Emperor Napoleon III. (Author's collection)

Here Napoleon initially lived in reasonable comfort, but circumstances rapidly changed upon the arrival of a new governor, Sir Hudson Lowe, who came to enforce stricter rules on his captive's conditions of residence, including Lowe's refusal to address Napoleon as 'Your Majesty', but rather only as 'General Bonaparte'. On the basis that the British Government had never recognized Napoleon's self-proclaimed title of Emperor of the French and, moreover, that his abdication had in any event put paid to any further right to expect this form of address, Lowe withheld all correspondence bearing an imperial or royal title and meant for Napoleon, whose own communications to the outside world Lowe scrupulously censored. In response, an indignant and increasingly depressed Napoleon refused to leave his residence, except to perform some occasional gardening, and his previously frequent rides and walks ceased as a protest against the interminable supervision imposed on him by his captors, who frequently and unnecessarily intruded into his room to verify his presence. Napoleon's regular complaints about these and other restrictions on his privacy and freedom of movement went unheeded.

His confinement did not go entirely wasted, however, for he began to dictate his memoirs to members of his entourage, particularly to Las Cases, who duly recorded recollections of his master's campaigns, his thoughts on strategy and war, his views on his adversaries, and conclusions reached on his successes and failures. Napoleon's testimonials contained a mixture of fact and exaggeration, but in them he demonstrated enough sense and perspicacity to admit that the invasions of Spain and Russia had constituted fatal errors. The compositions thus left behind ultimately formed the basis of the Napoleonic legend that swept through France in the course of the 19th century, recasting the Emperor as a political and social reformer rather than a tyrant bent on Imperial glory. Literature and biographies on Napoleon, and not merely those of French authorship, appeared rapidly and voluminously, almost unerringly portraying their subject in hagiographic terms – inheritor and consolidator of the great principles of the French Revolution, framer of the Napoleonic Code,

Above: Royal Navy officers aboard HMS *Bellerophon* cast quizzical looks at the Emperor after his surrender to British authorities in July 1815, the last of many miscalculations which landed him not as an exile in Britain but as a prisoner confined thousands of kilometres away. (Author's collection)

educational reformer and defender of the rights of the common man – as well as history's most accomplished commander.

Napoleon was to survive captivity on St Helena for only six years, for his health declined rapidly, characterized first with weight gain, lethargy and, increasingly, vomiting and a bowel disorder. He died on 5 May 1821, probably from stomach cancer – this was the conclusion of the autopsy performed on his body – or possibly arsenic poisoning, either deliberately administered or

the result of the build-up of this toxin, commonly present in the types of medicine prescribed to him, but furnished with no malicious intent. He was buried on the island in a simple grave that remained undisturbed until 1840 when, at the height of the Napoleonic craze, the French Government recovered his remains, brought them to Paris amidst extraordinary pomp, and interred them in Les Invalides, where they remain today.

A LIFE IN WORDS

Professor Felix Markham in his *Napoleon and the Awakening of Europe* (1965) asserted that 'Historians of Napoleon are apt either to be fascinated into adulation by his personality or repelled by the spectacle of the millions of lives sacrificed to his ambition…' With these words he succinctly summed up the bias characterizing most of the vast body of literature, now exceeding 100,000 volumes and focusing on Napoleon in all his guises – commander, head of state, and legal and social reformer – which began during the Consulate and continues to add to the inexhaustible fascination for the subject today. The most influential work of this early period, and which properly inaugurated the Napoleonic legend in print form, assumed the form of conversations during his imprisonment with the comte de Las Cases, among others, in which Napoleon reinterpreted his career to depict himself as the guardian of liberty and equality. This propaganda and apologia, worthy of the Stalinist era, emerged two years after Napoleon's death as *La memorial de Saint-Hélène* (1823), establishing a tradition of hagiography that continued well into the 20th century.

The Napoleonic legend, which admirers developed even during his lifetime in the form of imperial propaganda – bulletins, prints, medals and most of all paintings, especially by artists of heroic genre such as David and Gros. Romantic novelists like Alexandre Dumas and Victor Hugo contributed further to this trend until a powerful nostalgia had taken firm root by the 1830s. (Author's collection)

Still, in the first half of the 19th century Napoleon also had his detractors – and notable ones at that, such as Germaine de Staël, Chateaubriand and Benjamin Constant, who cast him as 'the Corsican Ogre' – but in seeking to render Napoleon's life as more akin to that of Charlemagne or Caesar than one of their barbarian opponents, such authors as Adolphe Thiers in his magisterial *Histoire du Consulat et de l'Empire* (20 vols, 1845–62), as well as a host of others described at best as admirers and at worst as sycophants, sought to portray him as the promoter of peaceful economic cooperation, and the heir and defender of the principles of the French Revolution. Indeed, to these and another two generations of French historians, the Emperor's reign was characterized by the unavoidable necessity of autocracy during a period when France required a 'strong man' to defend the nation against British machinations and the scheming Continental monarchs seeking to destroy the Revolution, whose principles challenged the inequality and feudalism on which the *Ancien Régime* thrived.

Nevertheless, if such flattery reached its zenith at the turn of the 20th century, an increasingly substantial and critical strain of historiography emerged after World War I, particularly from the Left which, doubtless influenced by the horrors of the trenches, viewed Napoleon as essentially the slayer of men in large numbers, responsible for instilling in French culture the militarism that somehow had made conflict in 1914 inevitable. These accusations did not, however, go unanswered; those of the Right rekindled the 19th-century characterization of him as the peace-loving, progressive ruler, whose authoritarianism, almost akin to fascism, was essential to prevent the breakdown of social order. Works by Ludwig (1924), Bainville (1932) and F. Kircheisen (1934) advanced such claims, while Madelin (2 vols, 1932–34), Lefebvre (1935) and Thiry in his colossal 28-volume treatment (1938–75) accomplished something of the same, though without a right-wing political agenda. British historians, writing on either side of the Great War, such as J. Holland Rose (1902 and 1912), H. A. L. Fisher (1912) and Herbert Butterfield (1939), maintained a grudging admiration for aspects of his career, unsurprisingly rejecting the narrow nationalism of their French counterparts.

The first proper attempt to assess Napoleon in an objective light came in the form of the Dutch historian Pieter Geyl's classic *Napoleon: For and Against* (1944), which gave voice to various French interpretations of Napoleon and his times, stimulating the avalanche of post-war reassessment that continues to this day. Some of this contains the partisanship of old, such as J. M. Thompson's unflattering biography (1958) juxtaposed with Jean Tulard's very favourable perspective in his *Napoléon ou le Mythe du Sauveur* (1977), which argued that the Emperor amounted to nothing less than a 'saviour' who supported the middle classes. But the mountain of scholarly evidence was by that time already mounting against the subject of these studies, with critics, particularly drawn from the Anglophone world, such as Christopher Herold (1962), Felix Markham

In a moving ceremony typical of his regime, Napoleon distributes eagles to his regimental colonels. Such symbolism, specifically designed to strengthen the bond between the Emperor and his soldiers, epitomized the neoclassical movement of the period which revived the traditions of Imperial Rome. (Author's collection)

(1963) and Corelli Barnett (1978), who, armed with plausible evidence, argued that Napoleon acted essentially for his own ends, in obvious contrast to Vincent Cronin's obsequious biography (1971).

Works of more recent vintage assess Napoleon with considerably greater objectivity and pass judgement increasingly on his capacity as a military commander – whose reputation hitherto remained virtually unassailable – as opposed to traditional assessments of man, reformer and head of state. Few historians dispute Napoleon's military genius, but literature in recent years has increasingly called into question the decisions he reached on campaign, particularly in the realm of grand strategy rather than of battlefield tactics. Such studies focus particular attention on his more substantial blunders, such as the invasion of Spain in 1808 and Russia in 1812. These are themes readily identified by historians such as Philip Haythornthwaite, Adam Zamoyski and a host of others. Some, like the eminent historian David Chandler, author of the groundbreaking, massive tome, *The Campaigns of Napoleon* (1966) and later *Napoleon* (1974), viewed him as 'great' but essentially cut from the wrong cloth, which is to say that while they admired his military achievements, they regarded him as more or less cynical and calculating, and claim that liberalism in Europe owed more to the Revolution than to Napoleon. Thus, while Chandler spared no words in admiring the Emperor's martial prowess and remarkable gift for generalship, he maintained that a spade must be called a spade: French expansion was about French interest – not about bringing the reforms of the Revolution for the benefit of the oppressed masses east of the Rhine.

At present we appear to have come full circle: the sycophantic works of the early 19th century now have their counterpart in works of the early

21st century in the form of two superb studies by Charles Esdaile, *The French Wars* (2001) and *Napoleon's Wars* (2007), whose very titles betray his position. Rather than the more traditional, collective, 'Napoleonic Wars', this academic shows his hand overtly: these were conflicts of the Emperor's own making – of his own ambition. Esdaile thus stands in sharp contrast to the diminishing number of advocates for Napoleon such as David Markham, who continue to cast the Emperor in the best possible light even while the weight of evidence continues to fall rather more on the side of Napoleon's detractors than on that of his supporters.

In assessing Napoleon on a purely operational level, most recent historians, stretching from Chandler – for more than a generation the great guru of Napoleonic warfare – to those of the last decade or two such as Robert Asprey, Philip Dwyer, Alistair Horne, Kevin Kiley, Geoffrey Ellis, Frank McLynn, Philip Haythornthwaite, Andrew Roberts and Andrew Uffindell, continue to applaud his military skill. Most would recognize the facility with which he applied such principles as the concentration of force, both at the strategic and tactical levels, the practice of living off the land, the focus on the enemy's weaknesses and the various forms of exploitation which so often contributed to Napoleonic success. All, in short, acknowledge that these remain key features of Napoleon's method of war and synonymous with decisive result. And while most scholars continue to recognize that Napoleon regarded war as being as much an art as a science, more than ever before argue that he waged it using a combination of old principles and others developed just prior to, and during, the Revolution, in combination with innovations of his own – thus undermining the traditional approach that attributes disproportional credit to Napoleon for being a tactical and strategic innovator, with little recognition offered to those who preceded him. David Gates (1997) and Owen Connelly (1987), rank prominently amongst such scholars. Nevertheless, assessments continue to be mixed, as revealed in contributions made by eight Napoleonic historians in their *Napoleon: The Final Verdict* (1996).

Napoleon personally laying a gun at the battle of Montereau, 18 February 1814, during the campaign in France. Trained as a gunnery officer himself, the Emperor recognized the battle-winning potential of artillery, while at the same time appreciating that it functioned most effectively in conjunction with infantry and cavalry – the practice known as combined arms. (Author's collection)

The debate thus shows no sign of abatement, with a steady flow of literature filling the shelves of bookshops and libraries, year upon year. On only one point do all sides agree: that Napoleon left on history a powerful and undeniable mark – political and social, as well as military – supporting Connelly's conclusion in *The Epoch of Napoleon* (1972) that no historian, 'even the most antagonistic, can deny that he was a true World Figure, whose work is still influencing our lives'.

FURTHER READING

Books on Napoleon and related subjects easily exceed 100,000 volumes, making the literature large enough to fill a substantial library unto itself. The texts below must therefore constitute but a sample of the best of the most recent, most general sources for study.

Barnett, Corelli, *Napoleon* George Allen & Unwin: London, 1978

Bergeron, Louis, *France under Napoleon* Princeton University Press: Princeton, 1981

Boycott-Brown, Martin, *The Road to Rivoli: Napoleon's First Campaign* Weidenfeld & Nicolson: London, 2001

Broers, Michael, *Europe under Napoleon, 1799–1815* Hodder Arnold: London, 1996

Brunn, Geoffrey, *Europe and the French Imperium, 1799–1814* Greenwood Press: Westport, CT, 1983

Butterfield, Herbert, *Napoleon* Duckworth: London, 1939

Chandler, David, *The Campaigns of Napoleon* Macmillan: London, 1966

——, *Napoleon* Weidenfeld & Nicolson: London, 1974

Chandler, David (ed.), *Napoleon's Marshals* Macmillan: New York, 1987

——, *The Military Maxims of Napoleon* Greenhill Books: London, 2002

Connelly, Owen, *Blundering to Glory: Napoleon's Military Campaigns* Scholarly Resources: Wilmington, DC, 1987

Connelly, Owen, *The Epoch of Napoleon* Holt: New York, 1972

Cronin, Vincent, *Napoleon: An Intimate Biography* Penguin: New York, 1971

Crook, Malcolm, *Napoleon Comes to Power: Democracy and Dictatorship in Revolutionary France, 1794–1804* University of Wales Press: Cardiff, 1998

Dufraisse, Roger, *Napoleon* McGraw-Hill: New York, 1992

Dwyer, Philip, *Napoleon, vol. I: The Path to Power, 1769–1799* Bloomsbury: London, 2007

Dwyer, Philip (ed) *Napoleon and Europe* Longman: London, 2001

Ellis, Geoffrey, *Napoleon* Longman: New York, 1996

——, *The Napoleonic Empire* Palgrave Macmillan: Atlantic Highlands, NJ, 2003

Elting, John, *Swords Around a Throne: Napoleon's Grande Armée* Da Capo Press: New York, 1997

Englund, Steven, *Napoleon: A Political Life* Simon & Schuster: New York, 2005

Esdaile, Charles, *The Wars of Napoleon* Longman: London, 1995

——, *The French Wars, 1792–1815* Routledge: London, 2001

——, *Napoleon's Wars: An International History, 1803–1815* Allen Lane: London, 2007

Esposito, Vincent J. and Elting, John, *A Military History and Atlas of the Napoleonic Wars* Praeger: New York, 1964

Fremont-Barnes, Gregory, *The French Revolutionary Wars* Osprey Publishing: Oxford, 2001

——, *The Fall of the French Empire, 1813–1815* Osprey Publishing: Oxford, 2002

——, *The Peninsular War, 1807–1814* Osprey Publishing: Oxford, 2002

Fremont-Barnes, Gregory (ed.), *The Encyclopedia of the French Revolutionary and Napoleonic Wars* 3 vols. ABC-CLIO: Oxford, 2006

Gates, David, *The Napoleonic Wars, 1803–15* Hodder Arnold: London, 1997

Geyl, Pieter, *Napoleon: For and Against* Yale University Press: New Haven, CT, 1949

Glover, Michael, *Warfare in the Age of Bonaparte* BCA: London, 1980

Grab, Alexander, *Napoleon and the Transformation of Europe* Palgrave Macmillan: London, 2003

Haythornthwaite, Philip, *Napoleon's Military Machine* Spellmount Publishing: Stroud, 1988

Haythornthwaite, Philip (et al.), *Napoleon: The Final Verdict* Weidenfeld Military: London, 1996

Herold, J. Christopher , *The Mind of Napoleon: A Selection from his written and spoken words* Columbia University Press: New York, 1961

——, *The Age of Napoleon* American Heritage Publishing: New York 1962

Hibbert, Christopher, *Napoleon: His Wives and Women* HarperCollins: London, 2003

Holtman, Robert, *The Napoleonic Revolution* J. P. Lippincott: Philadelphia, 1967

Horne, Alistair, *Napoleon: Master of Europe, 1805–1807* Weidenfeld & Nicolson: London, 1979

——, *How Far from Austerlitz? Napoleon 1805–1815* Macmillan: London, 1996

Kiley, Kevin, *Once There Were Titans: Napoleon's Generals and their Battles, 1800–1815* Greenhill Books: London, 2007

Johnston, R. M. (ed.), *In the Words of Napoleon: The Emperor Day by Day* Greenhill Books: London, 2002

Jones, Proctor (ed.), *Napoleon: An Intimate Account of the Years of Supremacy, 1800–1814* Random House: New York, 1993

Kauffman, Jean-Paul, *The Black Room at Longwood: Napoleon's Exile on Saint Helena* Four Walls Eight Windows: New York, 1999

Lachouque, Henry, and Brown, Anne S. K, *The Anatomy of Glory: Napoleon and his Guard* Greenhill Books: London, 1997

Lefebvre, Georges, *Napoleon* 2 vols Columbia University Press: New York, 1970

Macdonell, A. G., *Napoleon and his Marshals* Prion Books: London, 1996

Markham, David, *Napoleon's Road to Glory: Triumphs, Defeats and Immortality* Brassey's: London, 2003

Markham, Felix, *Napoleon* Weidenfeld & Nicolson: London, 1963

——, *Napoleon and the Awakening of Europe* Macmillan: New York, 1965

Marshal-Cornwall, James, *Napoleon as Military Commander* Barnes & Noble Books: New York, 1998

McLynn, Frank, *Napoleon: A Biography* Pimlico: London, 1997

Neillands, Robin, *Wellington and Napoleon: Clash of Arms, 1807–1815* Pen & Sword: Barnsley, 2003

Nicholls, David, *Napoleon: A Biographical Companion* ABC-CLIO: Oxford, 1999

Riley, Jonathan, *Napoleon as a General: Command from the Battlefield to Grand Strategy* Hambledon Continuum: London, 2007

Roberts, Andrew, *Napoleon and Wellington* Weidenfeld & Nicolson: London, 2001

Rogers, H. C. B., *Napoleon's Army* Leo Cooper: London, 2005

Rothenberg, Gunther, *The Art of Warfare in the Age of Napoleon* Spellmount Publishing: Stroud, 2007

Rothenberg, Gunther, *The Napoleonic Wars* Weidenfeld & Nicolson: London, 1999

Schom, Alan, *Napoleon Bonaparte* HarperCollins: London, 1998

Smith, Digby, *The Decline and Fall of Napoleon's Empire: How the Emperor Self-Destructed* Greenhill Books: London, 2005

Thiers, Adolphe, *History of the Consulate and Empire*, 20 vols Colburn and Company: London, 1845–62

Thompson, J. M., *Napoleon Bonaparte: His Rise and Fall* Basil Blackwell: Oxford, 1958

Tulard, Jean, *Napoléon ou le Mythe du Sauveur* Fayard: Paris, 1977

Wilson-Smith, Timothy *Napoleon: Man of War, Man of Peace* Carroll & Graff Publishers: London, 2002

Woolf, Stuart, *Napoleon's Integration of Europe* Routledge: London, 1991

Young, Peter, *Napoleon's Marshals* Hippocrene Books: London, 1973

INDEX